W9-CAE-117

LET'S
BE
LESS
STUPID

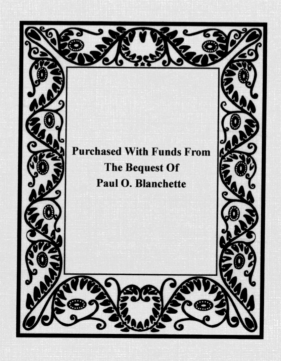

Purchased With Funds From
The Bequest Of
Paul O. Blanchette

LET'S BE LESS STUPID

An Attempt to Maintain My Mental Faculties

PATRICIA MARX

TWELVE

New York • Boston

SOUTH BURLINGTON COMMUNITY LIBRARY
550 Dorset Street
S. Burlington, VT 05403

818.54
MARX

Copyright © 2015 by Patricia Marx

All rights reserved. In accordance with the U.S. Copyright Act of 1976, the scanning, uploading, and electronic sharing of any part of this book without the permission of the publisher constitute unlawful piracy and theft of the author's intellectual property. If you would like to use material from the book (other than for review purposes), prior written permission must be obtained by contacting the publisher at permissions@hbgusa.com. Thank you for your support of the author's rights.

Bottom graph on page 129 courtesy of Lumosity.

Twelve
Hachette Book Group
1290 Avenue of the Americas
New York, NY 10104

HachetteBookGroup.com

Printed in the United States of America

RRD-C

First Edition: July 2015
10 9 8 7 6 5 4 3 2 1

Twelve is an imprint of Grand Central Publishing.
The Twelve name and logo are trademarks of
Hachette Book Group, Inc.

The Hachette Speakers Bureau provides a wide range of authors for speaking events. To find out more, go to www.hachettespeakersbureau.com or call (866) 376-6591.

The publisher is not responsible for websites (or their content) that are not owned by the publisher.

Library of Congress Cataloging-in-Publication Data

Marx, Patricia (Patricia A.)
    Let's be less stupid : an attempt to maintain my mental faculties / Patricia Marx.
        pages cm
    ISBN 978-1-4555-5495-9 (hardback) — ISBN 978-1-4789-8343-9 (audio download) —
ISBN 978-1-4555-5494-2 (ebook) 1. Aging—Humor. 2. Middle age—Humor.
I. Title.
    PN6231.A43M32 2015
    818'.5402—dc23

2015010743

SOUTH BURLINGTON COMMUNITY LIBRARY
550 Dorset Street
S. Burlington, VT 05403

For Deb Futter, Gordon Lish, and Susan Morrison
(whose combined IQs total 1473)

Contents

Prologue

Want to know how stupid I used to be? Before writing this book, I took an online IQ test consisting of twenty-one questions. "Which one of the five is least like the others?" asked the opener. The choices were dog, mouse, lion, snake, and elephant. Another item presented this critical state of affairs: "Mary, who is sixteen years old, is four times as old as her brother. How old will Mary be when she is twice as old as her brother? (a) 20 (b) 24 (c) 25 (d) 28." Then there were—as there invariably are—numerical sequences, such as this one that requires you to fill in the missing number: "8, 27, ?, 125, 216"—and a genealogical question about people who patently changed their names at Ellis Island ("If all Bloops are Razzies and all Razzies are Lazzies, then all Bloops are definitely Lazzies—true or false?"). One last example: "Which of the figures below the line of drawings best completes the series?"

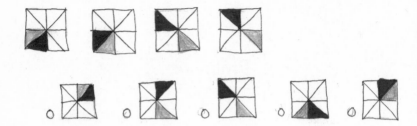

I knew that IQ tests online have been reported to yield generously higher scores than the professional models (by twenty-eight points, reckons one study), but even so, I thought, aren't these questions suspiciously manageable? (The answers are b, 64, true, and e). Or maybe my mother was right and I'm brilliant after all, I concluded as I cockily clicked to learn the verdict... which was...get ready: "You have an IQ of seventy-four." Seventy-four! This is a score that falls into the category described as "low intelligence." With a score like this, who would have predicted I'd be able to put on my socks unassisted? Apparently the test was timed, a detail I did not grasp when I periodically interrupted my testing to, oh, have lunch and do a few errands, such as voting for the next mayor of New York. This is not an excuse. Any idiot who cannot read the directions deserves an IQ that is a few points shy of "mentally inadequate." Morally I'm not so adequate, either, but that's another book (*Let's Be Less Debauched*).

I don't even listen to directions when I ask for them—and I ask for them all the time because honestly, in order for me to figure out which way is west, I must place a mental map of the United States in my noggin and then think, "California is left and California is west so ipso facto..." As soon as whomever I've accosted for navigational help starts up with "After you go under the underpass, take a left but not a sharp left, and keep going straight until you come to a building with an awning..." my mind is off in another world, mulling over what I should have for lunch because, let's face it, the real reason I ask directions is to be reassured that it's possible to get there and that someone exists who knows how.

Yet here I am, about to give you a few pointers on how to read this book. (Hey, if you want to be the author instead of me, who's stopping you from writing your own book?) First of all, please know that this is not one of those books like *The Decline and Fall of the Roman Empire* or *How to Install a Small to Mid Size Solar & Wind Power Generation System*, in which chronology matters. In these pages you will find a higgledy-piggledy assortment of highfalutin science, lowfalutin science, tests to find out just how stupid you are, exercises designed to make you smarter, games to amuse you, games to amuse me, drawings of the contents of my skull as rendered by someone (me) who can't draw, and accounts of me doing everything from learning Cherokee to zapping electricity into my head, all in an attempt to jump off the cognitive escalator heading downward to you-know-where. Both before and after my self-improvement regimen, I underwent MRI scanning of my brain and took a battery of IQ tests—real ones administered by a psychologist (who read the directions aloud to me). If you want to know the results right now, turn to the last chapter. (Don't tell my publisher I told you this. Let's keep it between the two of us.)

This book, then, is not only a primer of neuroscience (a sub-primer, I admit), a memoir, a self-help guide, a humor book, and a collection of brainteasers and quizzes, but also a suspense tale. If you are looking for a maritime history or picaresque novel, please go elsewhere.

"I don't know how to spell. Or they don't."

Cathy Schine

JULIE: The reason you can't adopt a Boston terrier in Massachusetts is because the laws are so...you know, so...what's the word for when something's extremely strict...you know...it begins with a *v*?
CLAUDIA: Draconian?
JULIE: Yes.

Julie Klam

"If I could remember the things I forgot I wouldn't have a memory problem, then, would I?"

Lynn Grossman

"When someone asks you something and you can't remember quickly, ask them 'how soon do you need to know?'"

Judy Siegal

"I've been washing my hair on and off, seeing if there was any appreciable difference in my own intelligence, concentration, etc. and I've noticed that if I don't wash my hair at all, or if I just rinse it that I feel smarter somehow....I do notice that if I wash my hair with bar soap I get the gain in intelligence but it's not as strong as what I would get if I didn't shower at all. . . . The only likely scientific explanation that I can give is that scratching my head/hair on a regular basis if I don't shower results in increased blood flow to that area, as a result I then get the increased intelligence from doing that."

Someone on the Internet

what is the word-
there-
over there-
away over there-
afar-
afar away over there-
afaint-
afaint afar away over there what-
what-
what is the word-

Samuel Beckett

What Is Your Mental Age?

DIRECTIONS:

You have two minutes to answer these questions. If you do not have a timer, start counting.

1. What's the word for the stuff you sprinkle on your food but it's not pepper? No, not salt but like salt but supposedly better for you because it doesn't have salt in it?

2. What's that thing that you put in the thing? The thing you take pictures with. *That* thing. What's the thing you put inside that?

3. What's the car that's not a Toyota Camry?

4. Who's the guy who isn't Robert De Niro?

5. What is the little plastic person you play with called?

6. How do you spell the drink that's made with rum, lime juice, and sugar and comes with a tiny umbrella, and don't act like you don't know what I'm talking about?

7. Do you need tomato paste or do you have some in the cabinet, and "I never use tomato paste" is not an acceptable answer?

8. Off the wagon? On the wagon? Which is the good one, and by good one, I mean the bad one that's not fun?

9. Remind me which is better: Baptist or Methodist?

10. What number is next?

11. Why is there a Post-it on the cutting board?

What? Why are there answers on the same page as the questions?! One explanation is that I trust you. Another is that if you wanted a sketch pad, you would have bought one.

ANSWERS:

1. NoSalt salt substitute. Mrs. Dash is also accepted.

2. Memory card. "Film" is not accepted. Get with it.

3. Honda Accord

4. Al Pacino. One-half point for Harvey Keitel or James Caan.

5. Barbie

6. Daiquiri

7. You are on the honor system.

8. I don't remember.

9. This was a trick question. Quaker. Half-credit for Unitarian.

10. Depends on how you define *next*.

11. I thought *you* put it there.

SCORING:

1 point for every correct answer.

    0: Older than the hills

  1–3: Same age as Father Time's uncle

  4–7: If you took your gray matter to *Antiques Roadshow,* they'd be impressed.

 8–10: Younger than springtime

   11: Will you write the rest of this book?

Chapter One

Welcome to My Brain

INSIDE PATTY'S BRAIN

Passwords... Calories consumed today...
Directory of women thinner than I am...
John? Jim? No, maybe a B name.
Bob? Brad? No, a King name.
Charles? Ed? No, Richard!
Richard?... Wedding presents
I owe... **SHOULD** have bought
apartment on Jane Street in
1990. **SHOULD** have become a
doctor. **SHOULD** have taken
Latin in high school. **SHOULD**
have paid attention in college.
SHOULD have ordered the halibut...
Connoisseur? Conoseiur? Connoseur?
Connoisieur?... The plastic thing on
the end of shoelaces is called an
aglet... Benjamin Moore paint swatches...

STUFF

NUTRASWEET
MEMORIAL of
DEAD
BRAIN CELLS

Available
space for
rent

What if I put the sofa in front of
the window and put the tweed
chair under the yellow painting and
moved the painting over the
fireplace and took the table from
the bedroom and put it where the
desk was?... Patty's wardrobe
1959- 2015... Headache or--
MAD cow disease ????...
"green acres is the place to be,
farm livin' is the life for me, land
STRETCHIN' out so far and
wide, keep Manhattan, just give me the
countryside." ... **RAGE** against
Verizon... If the economy is bad, then
inflation goes down, so then the Fed raises
rates so it's easier to borrow, so
BAD economy = GOOD for me... the time I
boldly introduced myself to Ed Muskie & told him I
knew his nephew & he said: "SO What?!"

First, meet my brain. It is the size of Kareem Abdul-Jabbar's fist, the consistency of flan, and weighs as much as a two-slice toaster. You probably think yours resembles a shelled walnut, but mine looks more like ground round with a high fat content. If you saw it at the butcher's, you'd ask for something a little less beige.

If you were a plastic surgeon, you'd say my brain needed a facelift. The reason my brain is so wrinkly and ridged is that, like a suitcase packed with a lot of junk, it contains too many neurons to fit smoothly inside my skull. If you ironed out my brain, you could use it as an ironing board cover.

Or you could use it to power your night-light. Do you know that operating a robot with a processor as fancy as your brain would require the same amount of energy generated by a small hydroelectric plant? You could not afford its electric bill.

Of late I've been a bit worried about it. My brain, I mean. Although the combination to my junior high school locker seems to be stored indelibly in some handy nook of my temporal lobe, right next to Motown song lyrics, could it be that elsewhere up there, not everything is in shipshape? When I ask my brain a simple, no-brainer question like "What is the word for that thing that's sort of a harmonica but more annoying and looks like you could smoke pot with it?" or "Who did that fat actress with those eyes and the diamond marry twice?" or "*Abjure* or *adjure*—which is the one I mean?" or "Did that lady say to turn left or right at the light?" or "The guy who just said hello to me—do I know him?"

or "Have I already told Phil and Cynthia this story I just started telling them?" or "All that stuff I used to know about Charlemagne's in-laws—where'd it go?" or "While I was looking at the fabric on the sofa in the background, did the villain in that scene get killed off?" or "What did I do last Saturday?" or "Did I turn

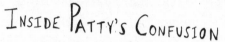

INSIDE PATTY'S CONFUSION

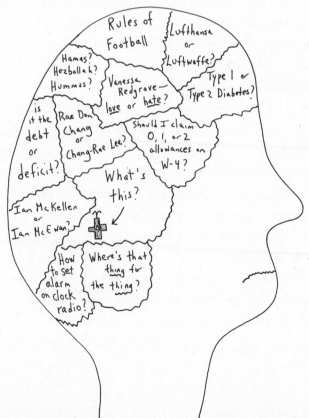

off my phone?" or "How in the world was I planning to end this sentence...?"

Anyway, what I believe I was going to say is that my brain is not nearly as quick on the draw as it used to be. Indeed, sometimes, when I look for my glasses while wearing my glasses, I think, "My, my, it's going to be a very smooth transition to dementia."

What is going on? In my darkest moments, I imagine that my friends are humoring me when they insist the amnesiac lapses of their brains are no less alarming than mine. ("Have you ever squeezed toothpaste onto your contact lenses?!" a friend asked triumphantly.) Could they be conspiring to shield me from my diagnosis, kindly reasoning the news would only agitate me since there is no cure for what my brain has? Another interpretation is that my think tank is filled with so much accumulated intelligence—the shoe size of my ex, the names of Sarah Jessica Parker's children, the calories in cottage cheese—that the contents are gunking up the works, not to mention leaving room for little else.

Or perhaps my brain simply has too much on its mind. How can it be expected to function when it must check my e-mail and texts every two to three seconds? Multitasking? It can hardly task. Back in the halcyon days when my cerebral cortex was in its prime, it had a cushy to-do list—a little homework, a few friends' names to keep track of, nothing more. Not even laundry to sort. Still another theory is that my brain was never the hot-shot I remember its having been. Was it ever really able to solve a polynomial equation? I think yes, but I can't make promises. (You don't think I kept a math diary, do you?) Furthermore, no matter what my upper story will tell you now, my habit for losing things goes back at least to my early twenties. Once, in a school cafeteria, I frantically asked all servers and eaters and cleaner-uppers in sight whether they'd seen my large black tote that, unbeknownst to me, I was conspicuously toting under my arm. I got funny looks, but nobody broke the truth to me.

Then there's the saddest possibility yet: Maybe noth-ing's the matter with my gray matter. Except for age. CORRECTION: second-to-saddest.

My brain is no spring chicken. It is as old as the wait for Godot, the hydrogen bomb, and Methuselah's great-great-great-great-great-great-great-great-great-great- great- great- great- great- great- great- great- great-great-great-great-great-great-great-great-great- great-great-great-great-great-great-great-great-great- great-great-great-great-great-great-great-great-great- great-great-great-great-great-great-great- (and so on and so forth) grandniece. How old exactly does this make my brain? Do I have to say? My mother would disapprove. On my last birthday, she said she remembered turning my age and feeling sorry for her mother for having a daughter so old. On the bright side, my mother still remembers. Her mother, my grandmother, remembered most things until she died at age ninety-nine, except she thought she was ninety-seven because, as we later determined, she forgot she'd lied about her age.

Will Reading This Book Kill You?

It is possible that you will become so immersed in solving the puzzles in this book that you will lose all sense of time, forget to eat, and eventually starve to death. It is also possible that page thirty-two will give you a paper cut that will become infected and the infection will turn into flesh-eating disease and you will be dead before you can say, "Page thirty-two." Or perhaps you will be so startled by what I have to say your heart will say whoa and you will keel over for good. This is all possible, but it is not probable. In fact, the odds of dying from complications of this book are one in 233,457,830.

DIRECTIONS:

Below are several other unlikely ways of dying. To be fair (to fate), they are arranged alphabetically. Number them with number one being the most farfetched.

__ Asteroid

__ Bus crash

__ Cancer

__ Car accident

__ Drowning in bathtub

__ Fairground accident

__ Falling coconut

__ Falling off a ladder

__ Falling out of bed

__ Food poisoning

__ Heart attack or stroke

__ Left-handed people using a right-handed product

__ Lightning

__ Plane crash

__ Radiation leaked from nearby nuclear power station

__ Scalding tap water

__ Shark attack

__ Snakebite

__ Terrorist attack

__ Train crash

__ Work accident

ANSWERS:

_1_   Shark attack: 1 in 300,000,000

_2_   Fairground accident: 1 in 300,000,000

_3_   Falling coconut: 1 in 250,000,000

_4_   Asteroid: 1 in 74,817,414

_5_   Bus crash: 1 in 13,000,000

_6_   Plane crash: 1 in 11,000,000

_7_   Lightning: 1 in 10,000,000

_8_   Radiation leaked from nearby nuclear power station: 1 in 10,000,000

_9_   Terrorist attack: 1 in 10,000,000

_10_ Scalding tap water: 1 in 5,000,000

_11_ Left-handed people using a right-handed product: 1 in 4,400,000

_12_ Snakebite: 1 in 3,500,000

_13_ Food poisoning: 1 in 3,000,000

_14_ Falling off a ladder: 1 in 2,300,000

_15_ Falling out of bed: 1 in 2,000,000

_16_ Drowning in bathtub: 1 in 685,000

_17_ Train crash: 1 in 500,000

_18_ Work accident: 1 in 43,500

_**19**_ Car accident: 1 in 8,000

_**20**_ Cancer: 1 in 5

_**21**_ Heart attack or stroke: 1 in 2.5

SCORING:

To compute your score, calculate the difference for each item between the number you assigned it and its actual number. Now add up these results. Or have your bookkeeper do this. If you received a score of 15 or less, you are immortal.

Middle-Age Mad Libs

DIRECTIONS FOR THE ONE PERSON WHO HAS NEVER HEARD OF *MAD LIBS*:

Ask someone how to play.

1. What Did You Do Last Night?

Three-syllable noun _____

Long word _____

Large household appliance _____

Three-syllable verb ending in -*eer* _____

Science word _____

Preposition _____

Conjunction _____

Last night? When was last night? I, uh…what *did* I do? Hold on, lemme look it up in my whatchamacal-lit, _____ [THREE-SYLLABLE NOUN]. Uh-oh, where's my—don't tell me I left it in the back seat of the _____ [LONG WORD]? Oh. Here it is. How'd that get inside my _____ [LARGE HOUSEHOLD APPLIANCE]? Anyway, we went out with the whats-theirnames. He works with whosis and she's the one with the brother. The brother went to jail for, what's it called? _____ing [THREE-SYLLABLE VERB ENDING IN -*EER*]? We went to that movie that's very popular but nobody likes. Called maybe _____ [SCIENCE WORD]? The suave guy who used to be in everything but now you never see him, he's in it. Didn't he direct that movie where people smoke? I think it has a _____ [PREPOSITION] or a _____ [CONJUNCTION] in the title. So, what'd you do last night?…What do you mean you and I had plans?!

2. Directions

One-syllable word ending in *k* _____

French-sounding word meaning "man about town" _____

Word you don't know the meaning of _____

Same word as above _____

Latin word, or, if you were not educated, a four-syllable word beginning with *m*

Remember when we used to go to Esther's? Not the first place, the second place. Start off like you're going there, but don't go that way. Go the other way. Stay on that until you come to that street we always miss. Make a right. Unless it's a left. You'll come to a _____ [ONE-SYLLABLE WORD ENDING IN *K*] in the road. It's actually more like a _____ [FRENCH-SOUNDING WORD MEANING "MAN ABOUT TOWN"]. Keep going. There'll be a tree on your left and then some rocks. Go past where the gas station used to be until you see a little, like, _____ [WORD YOU DON'T KNOW THE MEANING OF] thing. If you see a big _____ [SAME WORD AS

ABOVE] thing, you've gone too far. We're the house with the red _____s [LATIN WORD, OR, IF YOU WERE NOT EDUCATED, A FOUR-SYLLABLE WORD BEGINNING WITH M]. It's impossible to miss.

3. If Lincoln Had Lived

Unit of measurement, plural _____

One syllable, begins with *sk-* _____

Railings on a staircase _____

Place where nuns live _____

Adjective _____

Four, uh, what's the word? Four _____ [UNIT OF MEASUREMENT, PLURAL]? No. That can't be right. Four _____ [ONE SYLLABLE, BEGINS WITH SK-]? Four _____ [RAILINGS ON A STAIRCASE]? Anyway, that word plus seven years ago—or maybe even longer—in any event, our fathers brought forth on this—what's the thing called when it's not a country but it has countries in it? _____ [PLACE WHERE NUNS LIVE] or whatever. So, then, something something something and dedicated to the president. No, no, no. I'm the president. I think.

Dedicated to the—what? Wait a minute, wait a minute, it's a hard word and it's—does anyone know? Where was I? The important thing is that all men are, that all men are created _____ [ADJECTIVE]...

Back to my ol' noggin. What would it take to—poof—transform it into a spiffy young noggin? Back to the days when it was in tip-top shape? The days before the nuts and bolts and wires and connections inside my head started to slow down, shrink, get sidetracked, forget, become lazy, and go amiss in dreadful ways, but let's save the science for later? We're just getting to know each other's frontal lobes, and by *each other's* I mean *mine*. Here I just want to say that I would like a brain lift. Why not? If grown men can have bar mitzvahs, grandmothers can give birth, and Mick Jagger can sing "Time Is on My Side," then can't I have the mental prowess of someone who looks young enough to be carded, or at least someone qualified to think she will keep on thinking forever? There are a lot of neuroscientists who claim that cognitive rejuvenation is possible through a miscellany of interventions, ranging from exercising to eating sensibly to turning the photographs on your desk upside down to buying a piece of art that vexes you. Should I bring out the crossword puzzles? Learn to play bridge? Chew gum? Take a nap? Drink more coffee? Eat blueberries? Give up tofu? There are studies that tout the restorative benefits to the brain of each of these undertakings. There are also studies that say phooey to them all. How to proceed?

I would do just about anything for my brain. If you don't believe me, keep reading. But first...

Test Your Neuro-Knowledge

Can you figure out which of these facts I've made up? Answer true or false.

1. Women who have large breasts compared to their waists score higher on cognitive tests than do less curvaceous types.

2. In a sequel to *The Wizard of Oz*, the scarecrow worries that he has become *too* brainy.

3. We only use 10 percent of our brains.

4. Becoming rich can change your brain and make you less empathetic.

5. If a right-handed person wears an eye patch over his right eye for a week, his brain will remap itself and he will become left-handed.

6. Teenagers with IQs of 125 drink twice as many beers a night as those with IQs of 75 or less. (Could it be that the latter haven't figured out how to open the can?)

7. Drinking alcohol kills brain cells.

8. High school students with longer ring fingers relative to their index fingers have higher math SATs. Those who have a higher index-finger-to-ring-finger ratio do better on their verbal SATs.

9. Analytically minded folks tend to be left-brained, whereas artist types are more commonly right-brained.

10. Boys have bigger brains than girls.

11. Ears emit sound that can sometimes be heard by others.

12. *Pea brain* is not just an expression. A pea has a primitive neural tube that regulates the rate of transpiration and operates many of the plant's functions, such as photosynthesis.

13. If you made a smoothie by blending the contents of your brain, it would provide all the vitamins you need.

14. You have more thoughts on days when the barometric pressure is lowest.

15. There is a tiny region in the brain dedicated to passwords.

16. When a part of your brain is damaged, other parts can pitch in and take over.

17. People with higher IQs are more likely to be alcoholics.

18. The reason we turn down the radio in the car when we are lost is that we only have so much capacity for paying attention.

19. If you were to connect all the blood vessels in your brain, they would circle the earth four times.

20. The pathologist who removed Einstein's brain during the autopsy kept it with him in a jar for twenty years.

21. Learning is largely a function of growing new brain cells.

22. A study by Excedrin found that accountants get more headaches during the workweek than any other professionals.

ANSWERS:

1. **(T)** Women who have large breasts compared to their waists score higher on cognitive tests than do less curvaceous types.

2. **(F)** In a sequel to *The Wizard of Oz*, the scarecrow worries that he has become *too* brainy.

3. **(F)** We only use 10 percent of our brains.

4. **(T)** Becoming rich can change your brain and make you less empathetic.

5. **(F)** If a right-handed person wears an eye patch over his right eye for a week, his brain will remap itself and he will become left-handed.

6. **(T)** Teenagers with IQs of 125 drink twice as many beers a night as those with IQs of 75 or less. (Could it be that the latter haven't figured out how to open the can?)

7. **(F)** Drinking alcohol kills brain cells.

8. **(T)** High school students with longer ring fingers relative to their index fingers have higher math SATs. Those who have a higher index-finger-to-ring-finger ratio do better on their verbal SATs.

9. (F) Analytically minded folks tend to be left-brained, whereas artist types are more commonly right-brained.

10. (T) Boys have bigger brains than girls.

11. (T) Ears emit sound that can sometimes be heard by others.

12. (F) *Pea brain* is not just an expression. A pea has a primitive neural tube that regulates the rate of transpiration and operates many of the plant's functions, such as photosynthesis.

13. (F) If you made a smoothie by blending the contents of your brain, it would provide all the vitamins you need.

14. (F) You have more thoughts on days when the barometric pressure is lowest.

15. (F) There is a tiny region in the brain dedicated to passwords.

16. (T) When a part of your brain is damaged, other parts can pitch in and take over.

17. (T) People with higher IQs are more likely to be alcoholics.

18. (T) The reason we turn down the radio in the car when we are lost is that we only have so much capacity for paying attention.

19. (T) If you were to connect all the blood vessels in your brain, they would circle the earth four times.

20. (T) The pathologist who removed Einstein's brain during the autopsy kept it with him in a jar for twenty years.

21. (F) Learning is largely a function of growing new brain cells.

22. (T) A study by Excedrin found that accountants get more headaches during the workweek than any other professionals.

Chapter Two

If I Knew Now What I Knew Then

In case you haven't noticed, our brains, which peaked, by most measures, at twenty-two, have likely been on a cruel slide since we were, oh, say, twenty-seven. Since then our speedball has been chugging along progressively slower, and over in the paying-attention department, things haven't been getting better, either. Nor has time been a friend to our "working memory"—i.e., the scratch pad in our minds that allows us to retain information long enough to manipulate it, for instance by calculating the tip on the taxi fare or remembering what question we are in the middle of answering.

The Rise & Fall & Fall
of Patty's Brain

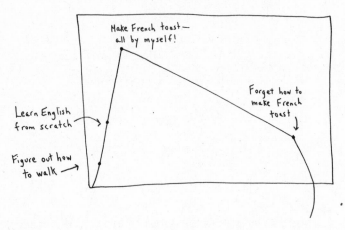

Make French toast — all by myself!

Learn English from scratch

Figure out how to walk →

Forget how to make French toast ↓

On the bright side, some neuroscientists such as Michael Merzenich say that the reason we lose our memories is not that our mental machinery forgets how to remember, but that it is representing the things we are seeing, hearing, and feeling less saliently than it did it in its heyday. When I talked to Merzenich over the phone, he told me about research showing that the slice of the world perceived by the average sixty-year-old is three-quarters the size of that perceived by a child; an eighty-year-old takes in only half of what she's capable of seeing. If life were a production of

Hamlet, you wouldn't see the ghosts overhead or the soliloquies to the side and forget about Horatio almost drinking the wine in the corner. Here is some of what else you're missing:

WHAT YOU MISSED
WHILE YOUR BRAIN WAS SLOWING DOWN

Money on sidewalk

← caviar

Hors d'oeuvres tray at cocktail party

Pope →   ← Mick Jagger

Celebrities in restaurant

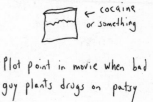

← cocaine or something

Plot point in movie when bad guy plants drugs on patsy

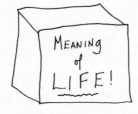

MEANING of LIFE!

How about wisdom? As we get older, aren't we supposed to acquire the common sense and sublime insight one otherwise must find embroidered on pillows? After testing three thousand sixty- to one-hundred-year-olds, some researchers at the University of California concluded so-called wisdom is merely the result of the brain's slowing down, becoming less impulsive and driven by emotion. Can't they come up with a wiser explanation?

What Was I Doing Upstairs That Made Me Decide to Go Downstairs?

You walk purposely toward the kitchen, bathroom, or Oval Office, and on arrival bewilderedly wonder, "Why am I here?" Did you come for a paper towel? Lip ointment? Are you supposed to sign the telecommunications bill?

Below are several brief scenarios. In each you wind up in a room, searching for something though you know no longer what. Select the most likely object of desire and provide an explanation to account for your choice. There may be several correct answers, but there is only one I have in mind. There are no incorrect answers, but one is more correct than the others. Do you know how to use telepathy? It could come in handy.

1. You are in your bedroom, talking to a friend on the phone. Now you are in your home office. What were you so hot to trot for?

    (a) Staple remover

    (b) Your friend

    (c) Datebook

    (d) Lint

2. In the den you turn on the television to watch your favorite program. During the first commercial, you put the remote in your pocket and run downstairs to the garage. Whatever for?

    (a) Fertilizer

    (b) Snow blower

    (c) Venison in spare freezer

    (d) Garage door opener

3. Uh-oh. Why did the lights go out? You make your way down to the basement, but um, what is it you are here to look for?

(a) *Flashlight*

(b) *Hand-crank radio*

(c) *Fuse*

(d) *Old Gladys Knight & the Pips album*

4. You are sound asleep, having popped one or possibly three Ambien a few hours earlier. Now you are in the kitchen. What is it you are so abjectly scrounging around for? (Can you hear me?)

(a) *Six-pack of hot dogs*

(b) *Twelve-pack of hot dogs*

(c) *Natural Balance Dog Food for puppies— Duck & Potato Formula*

(d) *More Ambien*

(e) *All of the above*

ANSWERS:

1. (c) Datebook. You are trying to make dinner plans with your friend, who wants to know if you're free Wednesday.

2. (d) Garage door opener. The batteries in the remote are dead, but luckily, the AAAs in the garage door opener will work, and you don't

need to drive anywhere before the end of the program.

3. (d) The album. The lights came back on— how else could you look?—and now it's time to paaa-rrrr-ty!

4. (e) All of the above. Everything is possible when you are on Ambien.

If you answered any of these correctly, you should tell me which horse to bet on at Meadowlands Racetrack.

What Did You Just Agree To?

You're walking down a noisy street and your cell phone rings. You can hear only snatches of what's being said by the caller—the reception is lousy. Nevertheless, you try to piece together the meaning of what's being said and carry on your part of the back-and-forth. You've surpassed the quota on the number of times you can say "What?" so you say, "Wow," and "That's great!" and "Unh-hunh." Later, in quieter times, it becomes evident that you've grievously misspoken. What was it that you said yes to?

Phone Call from Your Cousin

"...my favorite relative...perfect match...nobody needs two...fantastic...seven a.m., Tuesday...Mayo Clinic."

You agreed to donate a kidney.

From Guy You Went on a Bad Blind Date with Last Night

"So nice to meet...soul mate...forever...I don't believe it!...won't have regrets...minister or justice of the peace?"

Uh-oh. You promised to get married.

From Your Son

"...middle of semester...no refund...so could I?... Totally awesome....You're the best father in the world....Where's Thailand?"

Bankrolled by you, Bobby is dropping out of college to explore the sex industry in Thailand.

From: Caller ID Blocked

"...specially selected...one of five valuable prizes.... Act now or offer not good....Shipping and handling... expiration date?...Outboard motor not included."

Are you sure you want to buy a boat? Too late now.

Your Mother

"...leg hurts...not complaining....Shirley's son visits daily....Luke's old room?...Wouldn't be in your way....When?"

Lucky you. Your mother's moving in with you.

Your Creepy Neighbor

"My wife and I wondering...like adventure?... Get to know you better...hot tub...just us... protection."

You're such a swinger! Hope you like the couple next door.

Finally! Some great news about the bad news. Yes, our mental agility is no longer what it was in our twenties and thirties, but the reason for this, says Michael Ramscar, a linguistic researcher in Germany, is that we oldsters know too much. Our cerebrums are filled with more facts than are contained in all the editions of Trivial Pursuit. Another guy—not Ramscar but Daniel Levitin, who wrote *The Organized Mind: Thinking Straight in the Age of Information Overload*, cites a 2011 study that says on average, we absorb the equivalent of 174 newspapers' worth of information per day, which is five times the amount we sucked up in 1986. In the same way that it might take you longer to find that dry cleaning receipt in an overstuffed drawer full of odds and ends, so it might take you a long time to rummage through your gray matter before coming up with the name of that actress who was married to the guy from that show starring the one we thought was so funny—you know, from the gay thing? Ramscar programmed a computer to learn a certain number of new words and commands daily. He compared the computer's performance when it "knew" as little as a young adult to its performance when it had absorbed as much data as an older adult. The "older" computer had a slower processing speed: Ramscar chalked that up to its having more stuff to process.

And the stuff just keeps a-comin'. Ninety percent of all the data in the world has been produced in the last two years. Six thousand YouTube videos are posted a minute—and that figure was computed in 2011; by now there's probably not a number high enough to convey how overwhelming it all is. Here's another cocktail party statistic: The amount of information we generate every two days is equal to the amount produced from the beginning of civilization until 2003. That factoid comes from Eric Schmidt, formerly of

Google, so you can partly blame him for all your mental clutter.

How to make room for new stuff to be overwhelmed by? Perhaps selective forgetting is the answer.

WHAT YOU NO LONGER NEED TO KNOW

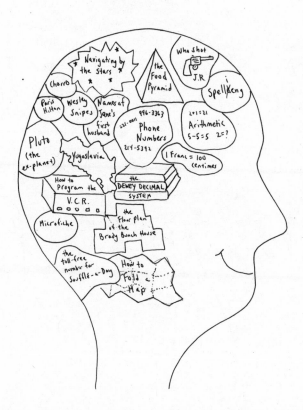

UNREMEMBER EVERYTHING
YOU LEARNED AT SCHOOL

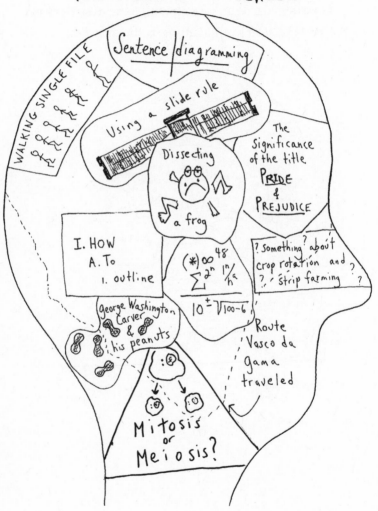

PRESIDENTS TO FORGET

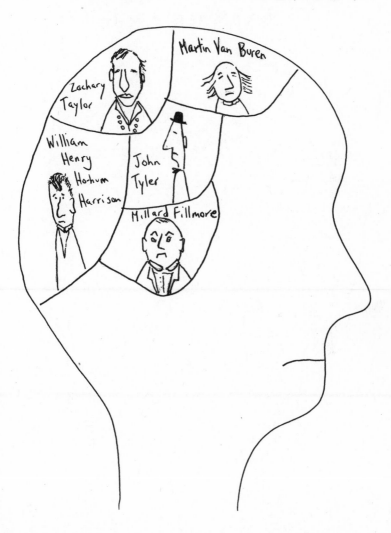

WARS YOU DON'T NEED
TO BOTHER ABOUT

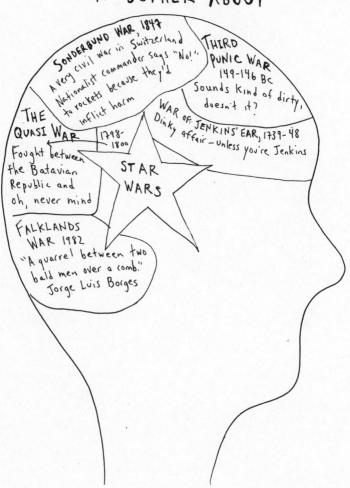

SONDERBUND WAR, 1847
A very civil war in Switzerland
Nationalist commander says "No!"
to rockets because they'd
inflict harm

THIRD
PUNIC WAR
149-146 BC
Sounds kind of dirty,
doesn't it?

THE
QUASI WAR
1798-1800
Fought between
the Batavian
Republic and
oh, never mind

WAR of JENKINS' EAR, 1739-48
Dinky affair — unless you're Jenkins

STAR
WARS

FALKLANDS
WAR 1982
"A quarrel between two
bald men over a comb."
Jorge Luis Borges

SHAKESPEARE PLAYS
YOU NEVER HAD TO KNOW ABOUT
IN FIRST PLACE

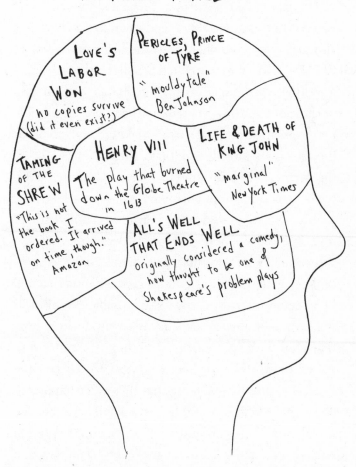

LOVE'S LABOR WON
no copies survive (did it even exist?)

PERICLES, PRINCE OF TYRE
"mouldy tale" Ben Johnson

TAMING OF THE SHREW
"This is not the book I ordered. It arrived on time, though."
Amazon

HENRY VIII
The play that burned down the Globe Theatre in 1613

LIFE & DEATH OF KING JOHN
"marginal" New York Times

ALL'S WELL THAT ENDS WELL
Originally considered a comedy, now thought to be one of Shakespeare's problem plays

*   *   *

Yes, it is an assuagement and a palliative to know that at least until the age of sixty, our vocabulary augments and enhances itself as we peregrinate and wend our way into senectitude, senescence, and sesquipedalianitis. It is also nice that in our olditude we are better at big-picture thinking and more empathetic. Still, by the advanced age of twenty there is a very good chance that the pre-frontal cortex—the real brains of the brain, responsible for problem-solving, decision-making, and complex thought—has already begun to shrivel. Humans, by the way, are the only animals whose brains are defini-tively known to atrophy with age and—yay us again—we are also sui generis in suffering from Alzheimer's disease. (Recent studies suggest that cats may also be susceptible, which would make them as dotty as some of their owners.) As distinctions go, dementia may not be as monumental as, say, the opposable thumb. It is not, however, necessarily the first episode in a story that ends with your caregiver finding the butter dish in the drawer of your bedside table. To tell you the truth, I'm not guaranteeing that this won't happen to you—genes being what they pigheadedly are. For the time being, there's nothing that can be done to prevent Alzheimer's, but in the last few years, scientists and entrepreneurs have been claiming there may be measures you can take to minimize, slow down, or even reverse cognitive decline.

They would not have said this as recently as a few decades ago. Then, most biologists would have told you that your brain is fully formed during childhood and, like a photograph after it's been developed, is doomed to degrade thereafter with neurons (nerve cells) fading like pigment on paper until you succumb to senility. Forget senility. Today we regard Alzheimer's and other dementias as diseases rather than as consequences of normal aging. Moreover, we now consider the brain to be as labile as a digital image in the hands of a Photoshop fiend. The three-pound wrinkly glop of glopoplasm in your skull contains about a hundred billion neurons, one for every human being who ever be'd. Each neuron can hook up with up to ten thousand others (polygamy-style, not serially monogamously). Hence there are at least one hundred trillion neural connections in your brain, which is more than there are stars in the Milky Way galaxy, but who's counting.

Not only does the brain have a lifelong ability to create new neurons; like a government with an unlimited highway budget, it has an endless capacity to build new roadways. Networks of linked neurons communicate chemically and electrically encoded data to one another

(*Hey, neuron, pass it on: That stove is hot!*) at junctures called *synapses*. Fresh neural trails are generated whenever we experience something new—learn the tango, try a liverwurst canapé, take a different route to work. Repeat the activity and the pathway will be reinforced. This is why London cabbies, whose job requires them to memorize a mesh of twenty-five thousand streets and thousands of landmarks, were found to have larger hippocampi than the city's bus drivers, who are responsible for learning only a few routes. The hippocampus plays a major role in memory formation. This is also why certain regions of the brains of bilinguals are bigger than the corresponding regions of monolinguals, *verstehen sie mich?*

PARKING LOT FOR BAD DRIVERS

At the parking lot for bad drivers, you are not allowed to park in a spot that is next to two occupied spots. In other words, no three cars can be contiguous— vertically, horizontally, or diagonally. This cuts down on accidents, and gives everyone ample room to get in and out of their vehicles and to dump their shopping carts willy-nilly instead of properly returning them to the drop-off areas. How many cars can the lot fit?

ANSWER: 16

*   *   *

(Hey, monolinguals, don't feel bad. Bilinguals are frustrated by more tip-of-the-tongue moments than you are. It is theorized that similar-sounding words get in the way of each other in the retrieval process, and since bilinguals know twice as many words, this is a greater hazard for them. Another theory is that words used less frequently than more popular words like *the* and *wine* are stored in harder-to-reach nooks and are therefore more elusive. Bilinguals, having accumulated all those words, must stash them away on the tippy-top shelves of their closets. Even deaf people who communicate with sign language have trouble fetching words from their mental dictionaries. Their glitches are called—can you guess?—tip-of-the-finger moments.)

The ability of the brain to reorganize itself as a result of learning and new experience is called *plasticity*. My typing this sentence, for instance, changed my neural wiring, and your reading my words changed yours. Reading a novel, new research has found, may cause heightened connectivity in the brain that could last five days. There is good plasticity and bad plasticity. If, say, you don't keep up with your Urdu lessons, the Urdu-y connections in your superior temporal gyrus will become far less superior, and before long you won't even be able to order a glass of water in Urdu.

The notion that we can affect the resilience of our brains by investing in it early on, banking mental health as if in a 401(k)—to borrow an analogy from the psychologist Sherrie All—hinges on the widely accepted theories of *brain reserve* and *cognitive reserve*. Kenneth Kosik, a neurologist and neuroscience professor at the University of California at Santa Barbara, explained these two kindred concepts to me during a rapid discourse that he called "The History of Alzheimer's in Thirty Seconds," which lasted about half an hour. Here's the short version: In 1988, autopsies of several elderly people revealed the plaques and tangles associated with Alzheimer's disease. However, these individuals, during their lifetimes, had displayed no signs of dementia. It has been hypothesized that they'd been buffered from the effects of the disease by the extra neuronal capacity that they had been born with (brain reserve) or accrued through years of intellectual and physical pursuits (cognitive reserve). Similarly, a study that analyzed the essays written by 678 elderly nuns when they were in their twenties found that the sisters who had used the most linguistically complex sentences were the least likely to have Alzheimer's, which is why I've added this unnecessary subordinate clause even though it's been a long time since I was in my twenties.

How is it that certain minds seem able to forestall senescence despite genetic programming? The damage to the
brain caused by Alzheimer's can be compared to traffic
jams caused by tractor-trailer accidents. Someone who
has a robust neural network can find ways around these
obstructions using back roads.

But not forever. Unless you have the good luck to
kick the bucket before your roadways become disas-
trously clogged up, sooner or later, even you, with your
clever compensatory strategies, will have difficulty getting from here to there. Paradoxically, those with higher
IQs, more education, or higher occupation achievement
deteriorate faster than average once they show symptoms
of Alzheimer's disease. To wit (if I may use that phrase),
researchers found that every year of education postpones
the memory failure associated with dementia by two and
a half months, but once the pathology becomes apparent,
the rate of diminishment is 4 percent faster.

Left or Right, Up or Down?

You were born with a sense of direction. I don't mean
that as soon as you plunked out of the birth canal you
could find your way from the maternity ward to the

gift shop—or even that your innate wherewithal is as sophisticated as that of a lobster, fruit fly, or bacterium. Still, like a new toy with batteries included, your hippocampus and entorhinal cortex came equipped with navigational neurons, though not all of them fully formed. The first to mature were *directional cells*, which tell you which way you are facing. Next to develop were *place cells*, which enable you to memorize landmarks; and finally, after you became mobile enough to explore hither and thither, your *grid cells* evolved, allowing you to keep track of your path by creating a mental map of your surroundings.

Whether you proceed from A to B by remembering to turn left at the 7-Eleven or by intuiting that after an eighth of mile you must go north depends on which cells are more commanding. In general, women tend to reference landmarks when moving through space, whereas men tend to rely on geometric clues, taking into account the lay of the land and estimating distances traveled. The method used by women requires a larger memory and results in their being less likely to be lost than men. (The average male drives an extra 276 miles a year because he doesn't know where he's going; a woman, a mere 256 miles.) By the way, if you are trying to find a woman with a good sense of direction, check her fingers. Scientists at MIT discovered that women whose ring fingers are equal in length to or longer than their index fingers are good at navigation (and can help you find the lost women). It is theorized that women with relatively long ring fingers were exposed to greater amounts of testosterone in the womb.

Language can also influence the way in which we get our bearings in the world. For example, the Aboriginal Pormpuraaw in Australia rarely use words such as *left*, *right*, *forward*, and *back*. Instead they talk in terms of *east*, *west*, *north*, and *south*. "I have a mosquito bite on my southeast leg," a Pormpuraaw tribesman might say, or "Could you pass the salt to your west?" As a result the Pormpuraaw have a much better feel than we do for orienting themselves in space. Or at least than I do. (Which way did you say the next page is?)

In any case, the more you practice your spatial skills, the better they become. Conversely, if you rely on your GPS device, your way-finding cells will wither and you will have to use your GPS even more.

DIRECTIONS:

How good is your sense of direction? Speaking of directions, these are so straightforward, you can figure them out. If there are four options, choose two; if there are two options, choose one.

1. You're in Australia, but hear a rumor that the grass is greener in New Zealand. You decide to find out. Which way do you go?
Left/Right/Up/Down

2. Uh-oh. Deported! They're kicking you out of the United States. Russia gives you asylum but not forever. Holed up in the Moscow airport, you hear that Venezuela will take you. Quickest route is which way?
Left/Right/Up/Down

3. You are a polar ice cap in Antarctica. Which way do you melt?
Up/Down

4. You are—OK, were—Osama bin Laden, holed up in your so-called safe house in Abbottabad, Pakistan. But, oops, you forgot your favorite comb near the Afghanistan-Pakistan border and your hair is getting gnarly. You command your lackeys to dig a tunnel. Which way?
Left/Right

5. You reside in Iowa Falls and read that Idaho Falls is one of the one hundred best places in the country to live—and also has great potatoes. You pack your car with all your

belongings and drive along roads pointing...
Left/Right/Slightly up/Slightly down.

6. You went to Timbuktu, and then realize
   you meant to go to that other place that
   nobody thinks exists: Transylvania. Your GPS
   recalculates, sending you...
   Left/Right/Up/Down

7. You are lost luggage. On your way from Paris
   to Beijing, you got shanghaied to Shanghai.
   You are put on another plane in Shanghai,
   this one allegedly headed for Beijing. You
   make sure the aircraft's nose is pointed...
   Left/Right/Up/Down

8. Manhattan's so passé. Move to Brooklyn
   before that becomes passé. Tell the Uber
   fellow to turn...
   Left/Right/Up/Down

9. You are, no offense, a slave ant, slogging away
   in an ant colony in Vermont. When you learn
   that the motto of New Hampshire is Live Free
   or Die, you make up your mind to flee to that
   land of promise. Which way do you crawl?
   Left/Right

10. You are in the land of the Munchkins, but
    need to be in the Emerald City. How to get

there? Follow the Yellow Brick Road. Yes, but this-a-way or that-a-way?
Up/Down

ANSWERS:

1. Right, down
2. Left, down
3. Up
4. Left
5. Left, slightly up
6. Right, up
7. Up, left
8. Down, right
9. Right
10. Up

SCORING:

0: Do not leave your house without a paid companion.

1–3: If you venture outside, leave a trail of bread crumbs.

4–6: If you are a Boy Scout, you deserve a merit badge in Space Exploration. While you're at it, award yourself a Pulp and Paper badge because there are extra.

7–9: You should teach a class instructing Pacific salmon how to swim from Hawaii to Alaska.

10: You are a homing pigeon.

Where in the World Are These French Fries?

So what if you don't know anything about geography? Nobody does around here. A British news team asked random Americans on the street to name a country that began with *U* and nobody came up with *United States*.

How much do you know about our global neighbors?

This is the only quiz that assesses your geo-cultural intelligence by measuring your potato aptitude. The directions are simple, even if the questions are not. Below is a list of ways in which French fries are served around the world. Your job is to identify the nationality of each tater. Next to each item is what I'd like to call a clue, but, as you may have already figured out, my drawing abilities are not good enough to be considered helpful. At the very least, the pictures should discourage you from answering "United States."

WHERE IN THE WORLD ARE THESE FRENCH FRIES?

	Presentation	Map	Country
1.	Topped with butter and sugar		_____
2.	Sprinkled with bacon		_____
3.	Mushed up with cheese curds and slathered with gravy		_____
4.	Seasoned with chicken salt		_____
5.	Dolloped with mayonnaise		_____
6.	Served with sheep's cheese and garlic sauce		_____

Presentation   Map   Country

7. Dolloped with mayonnaise   _____

8. Assisted with mint-coriander
    dressing   _____

9. Fancied up with
    remoulade sauce   _____

10. Disguised by hot mustard   _____

11. Hidden under a
    fried egg   _____

ANSWERS:

1. Vietnam
2. Philippines
3. Canada

4. Australia

5. Netherlands

6. Romania

7. Belgium

8. Pakistan

9. Denmark

10. Ireland

11. Spain

SCORING:

If you recognized any country other than Canada (so obvious!), you deserve to be secretary of state. If your only correct answer was Canada, award yourself the Department of Agriculture. If your score was 0, we must report you to the secretary of the interior.

Chapter Three

I Get Me Smarter Soon

OK, let's get back to me now. It's time to turbocharge my brain. During the next four months, I plan to cram my days and nights with as many brain-boosting pursuits as I can stand. If there's a shred of scientific evidence that a certain intervention might help, then it goes on my list. My list is very long and the bigwig in my head is very lazy (it takes after me). Not everything will make the cut. You don't really expect me to eat legumes and unrefined cereal, do you? Both are staples of the Mediterranean diet, which has been universally and tediously endorsed for its wholesome effects on brain function. And don't ask me to give up Diet Coke.

Liquid Capital

You thought the merlot tonight was expensive? Ho, ho, ho. Try ordering a bottle of Azature Black Diamond nail polish. At $250,000 for a half ounce, it would set you back $64 million for a gallon.

DIRECTIONS:

Order the entries below from most expensive to least, assuming you're buying a gallon of each and that you're not shopping for deals at Costco. This quiz is as much about critical thinking and unit conversions as it is about recalling your last trip to the grocery store, apothecary, or sperm bank.

__ Diet Coke
__ V8
__ Vodka
__ Scorpion venom
__ Scorpion antivenom
__ Mayonnaise
__ Paint (sienna)
__ Rockstar Energy Drink

__ Gasoline

__ Human blood

__ Bear blood

__ Nail polish

__ Cough syrup (medicinal)

__ Cough syrup (recreational)

__ Black ink for computer printers

__ Ketchup

__ Skim milk

__ Molten gold

__ Salad dressing (ranch)

__ Prison wine, aka pruno, aka white lightning

__ Holy water

__ FIJI bottled water

__ Wite-Out

__ Horse semen

__ Human semen (male)

__ Chloroform

__ Sodium thiopental, aka truth serum

ANSWERS:

1   Scorpion venom ($39,000,000)

2   Scorpion antivenom ($270,227.80)

3   Molten gold ($166,694.40)

_4_ Human semen ($108,154.57)

_5_ Sodium thiopental, aka truth serum
($26,676.54, not counting the plane ticket
for your drug mule)

_6_ Horse semen ($6,032)

_7_ Black ink for computer printers
($2,700)

_8_ Cough syrup (recreational) ($2,600 for
recently discontinued Actavis, the brand
most abused by Southern rappers)

_9_ Human blood ($1,500)

_10_ Nail polish ($890)

_11_ Wite-Out ($601.60)

_12_ Holy water ($435.20)

_13_ Chloroform ($239.36)

_14_ Cough syrup (medicinal) ($106.24)

_15_ Vodka ($100.69)

_16_ Salad dressing (ranch) ($43.52)

_17_ Mayonnaise ($38.27)

_18_ Paint (sienna) ($25)

_19_ Ketchup ($19.20)

__20__ Skim milk ($17.92)

__21__ Rockstar Energy Drink
($15.36)

__22__ V8 ($9.79)

__23__ Diet Coke ($8.67)

__24__ Prison wine, aka pruno, aka white lightning
($8)

__25__ FIJI bottled water ($7.68)

__26__ Gasoline ($3.76)

__27__ Bear blood ($0)

SCORING:

Use the same daffy method to score this quiz as for
"Will Reading This Book Kill You?" (page 9). Compare your ranking with the correct lineup. If you were
correct at least eight times, off by one at least nine
times, or off by two at least ten times, you are ready to
wean yourself from the bottle and introduce solids to
your diet.

Should you ease off the drinking in any case? Con-
trary to popular opinion, alcohol does not kill brain
cells. What's more, drinking boring, I mean moderate,

amounts of liquor protects you to some degree against age-related cognitive decline. According to a study done at the Catholic University of the Sacred Heart (where, yes, wine does stand in for the blood of Christ), 29 percent of those who never drank suffered from mental impairment versus only 19 percent in the merrier group. Alcohol does, however, damage dendrites—the branch-like neural ends that conduct electrochemical impulses from adjacent cells and carry them toward the cell body. If there is a problem with your dendrites, your cells will therefore have difficulty receiving messages from one another. It's like the Internet going down. But cheers: If you can just cut down on that copious amount of booze you've been consuming, the damage will undo itself.

Another thing you don't have to worry about: No matter what you may have heard during Prohibition, drinking will not lead to spontaneous combustion.

(I hate to end this on a down note, but some dipsomaniacs suffer from a neurological disorder called Wernicke-Korsakoff syndrome, which can cause confusion, memory problems, and other things you don't want, such as death. It does not come from alcohol per se but rather from a deficiency of thiamine [vitamin B_1], whose absorption by the body is blocked by alcohol.)

*   *   *

Like boozing it up, napping will also be absent from my get-smart-quick plan—even if scientists try to lull me asleep by alleging that during a siesta, the brain cleans itself up, consolidating short-term memories and trundling them over to long-term storage areas. I will keep my eyes open even if I am presented with evidence claiming that dozing off during the day would make me be more alert, remember more, be more focused, and have a greater sex drive. I will say that I don't care—maybe because, as studies have shown, after my existing on five to six hours of sleep a night for the past few decades, my decision-making skills are sorrily compromised. If these scientists are still awake, I will also let them know that a psychologist at the London School of Economics named Satoshi Kanazawa reported that people who go to bed later and get up later have higher IQs. Here are his findings regarding the bedtimes and wake-up times of the smart and the dumb as reported in *STUDY Magazine*, and only the unstudious could refute a publication by that name.

Very Dull (IQ < 75)
Weekday: 11:41 p.m.–7:20 a.m.
Weekend: 12:35 a.m.–10:09 a.m.

Normal (IQ between 90 and 110)
Weekday: 12:10 a.m.–7:32 a.m.
Weekend: 1:13 a.m.–10:14 a.m.

Very Bright (IQ > 125)
Weekday: 12:29 a.m.–7:52 a.m.
Weekend: 1:44 a.m.–11:07 a.m.

By the way, it is also true that acording to various studies, higher-IQ people are more likely to be left-handed, tall, thin, blue-eyed, oldest children who are atheist, liberal, prone to lying, drinking, and using drugs—and in ownership of a cat.

For the most part, the mind-building activities recommended by the cognoscenti meet all or some of the following criteria: They are intellectually challenging, physically demanding, socially engaging, or stress-reducing (according to these guidelines, a party-going, high-jumping Buddhist monk who likes to assemble IKEA bookshelves while focusing on his breathing should be verrrrry brilliant). Among the most popular suggestions for staying sharp are playing online brain fitness games, learning a new language or musical instrument, working out aerobically, joining a book club, and practicing meditation. Not all the advice is so boring and predictable.

Below is a list of self-improvement endeavors that purportedly vitalize your mind. I have culled them from various books and websites. Some I have invented. Can you figure out which ones are bona fide? (Answer true for the true ones and bullshit for the others.)

How to Be Brainier

1. Write backward with your weaker hand.

2. Rearrange your furniture.

3. Make your bed using the flat sheet for the fitted sheet and vice versa.

4. Don't step on the sidewalk cracks for an entire day.

5. Create "top one hundred" lists.

6. Join a cult and then give the leader thirteen reasons why you're quitting.

7. Take a slow day in which you do everything at half speed.

8. Eat dinner under the table.

9. Parallel park while blindfolded.

10. Take a baked potato out of the oven with your bare hand.

11. Make a pineapple upside-down cake right side up.

12. Keep a journal.

13. Avoid reading the newspaper or news websites for a week.

14. Donate one-third of your clothes to charity.

15. Eat less.

16. Drink water.

17. Take ginkgo biloba.

18. Don't take ginkgo biloba.

19. "Be."

20. Sit up straight.

21. Wash behind your ears.

22. Take a nap.

23. Play Tetris.

24. Go to a black-tie affair wearing something red.

25. Consume antioxidants daily.

26. Get rid of toxins by gargling with prune juice.

27. File for a divorce.

28. Question everything. Ask why incessantly.

ANSWERS:

1. (T) Write backward with your weaker hand.

2. (T) Rearrange your furniture.

3. (B) Make your bed using the flat sheet for the fitted sheet and vice versa.

4. (B) Don't step on the sidewalk cracks for an entire day.

5. (T) Create "top one hundred" lists.

6. (B) Join a cult and then give the leader thirteen reasons why you're quitting.

7. (T) Take a slow day in which you do everything at half speed.

8. (B) Eat dinner under the table.

9. (B) Parallel park while blindfolded.

10. (B) Take a baked potato out of the oven with your bare hand.

11. (B) Make a pineapple upside-down cake right side up.

12. (T) Keep a journal.

13. (B) Avoid reading the newspaper or news websites for a week.

14. (B) Donate one-third of your clothes to charity.

15. (T) Eat less.

16. (T) Drink water.

17. (T) Take ginkgo biloba.

18. (T) Don't take ginkgo biloba.

19. (T) "Be."

20. (T) Sit up straight.

21. (B) Wash behind your ears.

22. (T) Take a nap.

23. (T) Play Tetris.

24. (B) Go to a black-tie affair wearing something red.

25. (T) Consume antioxidants daily.

26. (B) Get rid of toxins by gargling with prune juice.

27. (B) File for a divorce.

28. (T) Question everything. Ask why incessantly.

I'm no mind reader (yet), but I bet you are thinking, it took her many years to become as stupid as she is, how can she expect to become much less stupid in four months? Isn't cognitive change gradual, you reason, even lifelong? I guess we'll see about that. In any case, I have no patience with patience.

In due course, we'll take stock of my mental faculties. Unfortunately, my life is not one that is rich in obvious and observable mental benchmarks. If I were a poker champ, I could tally my winnings after my cognitive makeover and compare them to my average intake; if I were a chess player I could chart my ratings; an air traffic controller, I could tell you whether I caused fewer accidents and if, over time, my near misses became more or less bloodcurdling. Instead I'm a writer who muddles measurelessly through life (grammur and speling miztakes some perhaps you can see changeing?). How, then, to evaluate my progress? I had planned to keep a forgetting journal, but—spoiler alert—this is as far as I got before I forgot to keep up the entries:

Put laundry in machine and never pressed start button.

There's someone I have to e-mail. It's urgent. Who is it?

Lady at makeup counter said, "I have mixed feelings about purple" and "Green is not a priority color for me." Made mental note to remember for possible future use. Remembered a day later!

Ditto when salesgirl at Club Monaco said, "I wasn't
a turtleneck person until I tried on the Julie turtleneck. Now I'm totally a turtleneck person." Am I
getting smarter? On other hand: How do I know
if I got quotes right?

Forgot to buy a new memory card.

Remembered the name Michael Keaton but forgot
why I was trying to remember him.

Unchartered territory? Uncharted?

How many times do I have to look up the word
eidetic?

Told someone I had to get off phone because I had
to look for my phone.

After I have finished bettering myself, I intend to ask
my friends whether they've detected any changes in
me. Of course, it's arguable whether anyone really pays
attention to the lapses of others. (Has anyone shared in
your joy when, after days of rifling through every hiding
place in your cranium, you finally came up with the
name of the actor who died shortly after he appeared in
One Flew over the Cuckoo's Nest? William Redfield, as
if you care.) There are, thankfully, more reliable, or at
least more objective, or at least other, assessment tests.
Before I begin my get-less-stupid program and then

again soon after I finish, I will have my head scanned in an MRI machine and also take a battery of IQ tests.

Thus: What's crucial right now, during this interval before my evaluation, is that I stay as pristinely and impeccably stupid as ever. No feeding from the tree of knowledge, not even any nibbling of trivia from the Dining and Wine section of the *New York Times*. My goal is to discourage the formation of new neural pathways and weaken the ones I have (good-bye trying *One Hundred Years of Solitude* again). Since our brains change all the time, even when we sneeze, do beadwork, or watch a cricket match, this is not a simple enterprise. Watching TV helps—and not the good kind that's reviewed.

Studies have shown that all sorts of external factors affect our short-term memory, or is it just that there are a lot of studies?

DIRECTIONS:

For each of the following, choose (*a*) if the item tends to make us forget, (*b*) if it tends to make us remember, or (*c*) if the item has not yet become the focus of grant funding.

1. The sight of other people's faces (*a*) (*b*) (*c*)
2. Deep voices (*a*) (*b*) (*c*)

3. Drinking water out of paper cups (*a*) (*b*) (*c*)

4. Using your hands when you talk (*a*) (*b*) (*c*)

5. Walking through doorways (*a*) (*b*) (*c*)

6. Cooking risotto (*a*) (*b*) (*c*)

7. Playing with your hair (*a*) (*b*) (*c*)

8. Wacky fonts (*a*) (*b*) (*c*)

ANSWERS:

1. (*a*) Faces are distracting. If you want to recollect something, look at the floor or dreamily into the far-off distance—or at least tell everyone to go away.

2. (*b*) Scientists at the University of Aberdeen found that the utterances of men with low-pitched voices were more memorable to women than anything squeaky fellows had to say.

3. (*c*)

4. (*b*) Susan Goldin-Meadow at the University of Chicago says (possibly with her hands) that making gestures disencumbers our working memories and allows us to retain facts longer. She demonstrated this in an experiment in which subjects had to explain the solution to

a math problem while remembering a list of items. Those who wave their hands all over the place while explaining were able to recall 20 percent more.

5. (*a*) Passing through this threshold (aka *event boundary*) gives notice to the brain that it should dump the inessential information it learned in the previous room in order to clear mental space for new inessential information. Anything deemed important, such as the fact that the room is on fire, is consolidated and moved into long-term memory. As the University of Notre Dame researcher who discovered this phenomenon (Gabriel Radvansky) told a journalist (not me), "Doorways are bad. Avoid them at all costs."

6. (*c*)

7. (*c*)

8. (*b*) Strange fonts, particularly ones that are hard to decipher, make us look more closely at the text and pay more attention to the material. Got it?

Chapter Four

Head Shots;
or, Lights, Camera, Magnets

Now get undressed," says Dr. K, a woman in a lab coat who seems to run the show at the imaging center (aka the Neuropsychology and Cognitive Neuroscience Lab at Stanford). I have come here to document my pre-improved brain so I will have a baseline for later comparisons and humiliations. Specifically, the spick-and-span white cylinder in the next room will provide both anatomical renderings of my brain as well as activity maps. The former are MRIs (magnetic resonance images); the latter, fMRIs (the *f* stands for *functional*, not *fabulous*).

No to the jewelry and makeup, I am told by the technician, another woman in a lab coat. Both (the jewelry and makeup, not the women in lab coats) could contain metal, and the magnetic field inside this contraption is so mighty (millions of times mightier than the earth's) that it can pull metallic objects such as bobby pins, keys, and pens out of the pocket of anyone in the room and turn them into North Korean magnet-seeking missiles that could cut off the pinky or worse of those in the way. (Even so, says the technician, some women cry when they learn they can wear no lipstick.) I once spent a day rooting through all the trash in my apartment building because I accidentally threw out a super-powerful, one-of-a-kind experimental magnet that had been lent to my boyfriend by the scientist who invented it, but that's another story (and one that didn't end well). After putting on a set of paper scrubs and cotton socks, I hop with diminished dignity onto the gurney-like bed attached to the MRI machine. The technician, who will soon run like a wildebeest into the control room, nudges me into the mouth of the machine until I am enveloped from shoulders upward inside its tubular chamber, which doesn't seem much wider than a piece of rigatoni. I am warned that I will have to remain perfectly still. (Studies show that men squirm more than women do when inhabiting an MRI machine. To find out why this is so, you could image the brains of men—that is, if you could get them to stay still.) Ixnay on feeling itchy, I think. Same goes for breathing. For entertainment there is the noise of the scanner scanning, which alternately sounds like a John Cage composition (Sonata for a Hammer in H-Flat) and the alarm at a nuclear plant signaling you to leave ASAP. Is this what it feels like to be a piece of paper about to be photocopied? No matter. The radio-frequency waves or maybe it's the head-restraining brace is making me tired, which is more than I can say for my bed.

If you want to know how an MRI scanner works, you should probably ask someone else.

Since I'm the one who has the book contract, though, here is the not-totally-inaccurate gist: On a most elementary level, the machine uses magnetic fields and radio-frequency waves to manipulate the hydrogen atoms in your body. Why hydrogen? Because water, you recall—if recalling is still in your repertoire—is H_2O, which means that each molecule has two atoms of hydrogen. Since each of us is basically a wetland (we're 57 to 75 percent water, if you want to be factual-like), we are awash in hydrogen, especially in our soggiest parts, called *soft tissues*. MRI, therefore, is good for looking at squishy moist brains, and not so good with dry-bone detail. Our hydrogen atoms are always spinning (for lack of a better metaphor) along an axis (for lack of a better metaphor), and under normal conditions (for lack of a better metaphor) they are very unruly, pointing hither and thither like deranged tops (for lack of a better metaphor). In the presence of a formidable magnetic field, however, most of the atoms sync up, each axis aligned with the others as if a god with OCD (deist metaphor) had set them in motion. When pulses of radio waves are directed at the body, a few of these atoms become temporarily jostled. As they relax back into their pre-pulse state, they emit a tiny radio signal. A clever magnetic trick is used to localize these signals, and even cleverer mathematics is used to convert these signals into an image.

What the image reflects is the relative densities of water contained in the soft tissues, and since these amounts are different in different tissues, an anatomical map is created. Got it? If you think you can do this with refrigerator magnets and a transistorized AM radio, you have another thing coming.

On to fMRI. This is a technique for gauging activity in different areas of the brain by measuring the influx of blood to those places. If your brain is working unduly, say, to figure out where the Food Emporium keeps the Clamato juice, then it will require more oxygenated blood to do the job. As you become a pro at finding the Clamato, your brain will be taxed less and there will be a reduced inflow of blood to the Clamato section of your brain (near the guava nectar section, no doubt). During an fMRI scan, therefore, you are usually required to perform a task or two. Doesn't that make it sound as if they force me to unload the dishwasher? Instead, the fun and games include an exercise in which I'm asked whether the cards displayed sequentially on the computer screen "follow the rule" (what rule they were talking about, I never figured out), and another in which I am asked to determine if the colored shape on view matches the one I saw one, two, and three screens previously.

So there I am nestled recumbent and semicomatose inside the abyss, when I hear through the intercom headset the voice of one of the women in lab coats saying that because of a glitch in the machine, they cannot continue to administer the fMRI. Just relax, she says. Relax? That can mean only one thing. "How big is my tumor?!" I think. Then I think: Can they see how scared my brain is? Not exactly. The two regions in the brain associated with emotion (the amygdalae) may indeed light up on the monitor, indicating that there's some sort of neural hullabaloo going on there, but as far as the observers know, I could be fretting about being found dumb.

Nobody's saying that my brain broke the machine, but after a three-hour hiatus, followed by a test run of the gadgetry using an empty bottle as the subject, I reenter the magnetic girdle. We complete the testing. No results will be revealed to me today, however, because, as it is explained, the images will make more sense when compared to the analogous ones we'll take four months from now. Or could it be that the ladies are on the phone with my doctor right now, letting him know about you-know-what.

As a souvenir, the technician left me with a picture of my beige matter.

This is not my brain. This is a piece of gum.

This is also not my brain. It is a tomato.

This is my brain. Can you find the Finger Lakes?

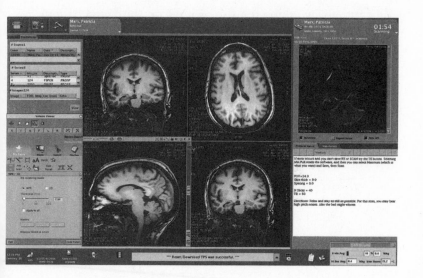

"What do you see?" I asked the technician apprehensively. "You have nice ventricles," she said. "It shows you're not schizophrenic. If you were, the ventricles would be all over the place." Even though this was not something it had occurred to me to worry about, I was relieved.

On the one hand, fMRI is a marvelous tool for looking at how we think, feel, see, and remember. On the other hand, those imaging portals at airport security are also kind of neat. Finally, consider this.

Several years ago, researchers at the University of California at Santa Barbara scanned a dead salmon, perfunctorily asking the fish as it lay on the fMRI patient table to identify the emotions being felt by various human beings depicted in a series of photographs. What did they find? You guessed it: Signals associated with thoughts were detected. (In fact, this was due to statistical error, but really, shouldn't statistics know better?) The researchers did not say what the dead fish was thinking, but my guess is, "I'd rather be lox."

Droodles

When I was a kid, I was intrigued by a paperback on my parents' bookshelf called *Droodles*, written by Roger Price in 1953. It was next to a book called *Thirteen Elegant Ways to Commit Suicide*, which amused me equally. That's for later. Droodles are simple and seemingly abstract line drawings—part doodle, part riddle—whose meanings are...you know what? It's easier to show rather than tell you. Here's an example of one of Price's Droodles.

What is it? Turn the page and find out.

It's a ship arriving too late to save a drowning witch.
Alternatively, it's a mother pyramid feeding her
baby. Here are three more. Can you supply a
brief description of each illustration?

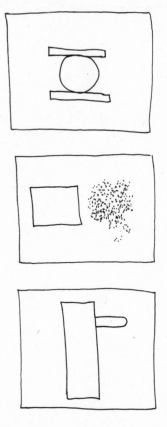

Turn page for answers. Deduct some points if you
hadn't already figured that out.

Give up? A tomato sandwich made by an amateur
chef, unassembled sandpaper, and a box
for Pinocchio, respectively. Deciphering a
Droodle requires what psychologists call
divergent thinking, or coming up with
multiple solutions to a given problem. The
phrase "divergent thinking" is a divergent
way of saying *imagination*. This ability to
think fancifully is not typically called on by
standard aptitude tests such as the SAT and
IQ. For this reason, Droodles can be used to
test creativity.

Below are nine Droodles (mine, not Price's). Come up with the caption for each, writing your answers in the lines provided.

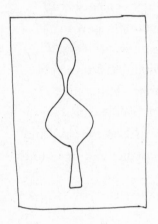
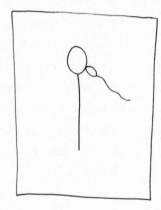

_____   _____

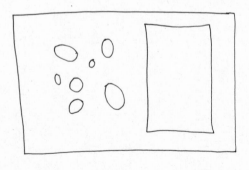

_____

Pregnant spoon

Sperm mating with a lollipop

Make-your-own Swiss* cheese kit

* Emmenthaler or Jarlsberg also accepted (as answers).

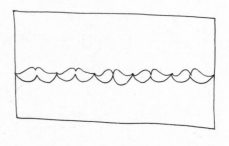

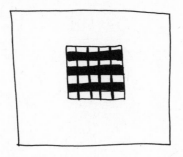

Prisoner seen through cell window

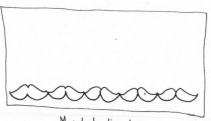

Moustache line dance

Jewish Easter bunny

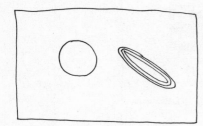

_____

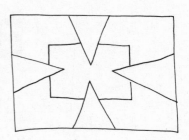

_____

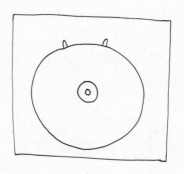

_____

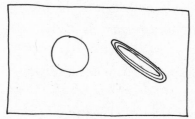

The divorce of Saturn

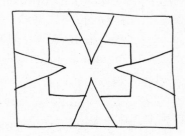

Four birds splitting the check

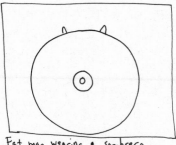

Fat man wearing a sombrero

SCORING:

1 point for each correct answer.

    0: Zero? Really? Do this test again, but this time cheat.

    1: Not everyone's creative. CPAs make a very good living.

2–4: Maybe you're more of a Rorschach type of person. Or maybe your strength lies in deciphering street signs.

5–7: Terrific job! This test was mostly fake, and yet you scored very well.

8–9: No effing way! I made up this quiz and there's no way I could get this close.

  11: You are likely a witch or a warlock. Do you have spells? Is that how you did this?

Chapter Five

My IQ, Part 1;
or, How Smart I Was Not;
or, In Search of Remembrance Now;
or, the Collected Stories of
Anton Chekhov

How Smart Are the Famous?

DIRECTIONS:

Match the person with the IQ. With a pencil.

SCORING:

Give yourself 6 points for every correct match. Add this to 100. Subtract 1 point for every match you get wrong. If you cannot do this calculation without a calculator, deduct 20 points.

Bonus points: Add the month, day, and year of your birthday. Reduce this four-digit numeral to one digit. Add your zip code. Divide by your niece's phone number plus the security code on your favorite credit card. Subtract your shoe size. Do the hokeypokey and turn yourself around.

Martin Luther	78	Galileo	155
Muhammad Ali	86	Jodie Foster	156
Thomas Edison	105	Andy Warhol	156
Johann Sebastian Bach	118	George Washington	160
Bill Clinton	118	Richard Nixon	160
John F. Kennedy	119	Voltaire	160
Lee Harvey Oswald	121	Ralph Waldo Emerson	160
Franklin D. Roosevelt	122	Sigmund Freud	160
Dwight Eisenhower	123	Stephen Hawking	160
Ulysses S. Grant	125	Leonardo da Vinci	165
Hillary Clinton	130	John Stuart Mill	165
Barack Obama	130–148	René Descartes	170
Ronald Reagan	132	Jean-Jacques Rousseau	170
Bobby Fischer	135	Plato	170
George W. Bush	137	Rembrandt	175
Gerald Ford	140	Madonna	180
Andrew Jackson	140	Napoleon	180
Arnold Schwarzenegger	143	Benjamin Netanyahu	185
Charles Dickens	145	Richard Wagner	185
George Eliot	145	Baruch Spinoza	187
Bill Gates	147	Quentin Tarantino	190
Benjamin Franklin	150	Jonathan Swift	200
Albert Einstein	155	Lisa Simpson	220
Reggie Jackson	155		

ANSWERS:

Martin Luther:	170	Galileo:	185
Muhammad Ali:	78	Jodie Foster:	132
Thomas Edison:	145	Andy Warhol:	86
Johann Sebastian Bach:	165	George Washington:	118
Bill Clinton:	137	Richard Nixon:	143
John F. Kennedy:	119	Voltaire:	190
Lee Harvey Oswald:	118	Ralph Waldo Emerson:	155
Franklin D. Roosevelt:	147	Sigmund Freud:	156
Dwight Eisenhower:	122	Stephen Hawking:	160
Ulysses S. Grant:	130	Leonardo da Vinci:	220
Hillary Clinton:	140	John Stuart Mill:	200
Barack Obama:	130–148	René Descartes:	185
Ronald Reagan:	105	Jean-Jacques Rousseau:	150
Bobby Fischer:	187	Plato:	170
George W. Bush:	125	Rembrandt:	155
Gerald Ford:	121	Madonna:	140
Andrew Jackson:	123	Napoleon:	145
Arnold Schwarzenegger:	135	Benjamin Netanyahu:	180
Charles Dickens:	180	Richard Wagner:	170
George Eliot:	160	Baruch Spinoza:	175
Bill Gates:	160	Quentin Tarantino:	160
Benjamin Franklin:	160	Jonathan Swift:	155
Albert Einstein:	165	Lisa Simpson:	156
Reggie Jackson:	160		

*   *   *

When I took the SATs in eleventh grade, my friend Judy advised me that if I stuck chewed cinnamon Trident chewing gum to the upper right-hand corner of the first page, I would get a perfect score. I did not follow her advice and I did not get a perfect score. After graduating from college, I considered retaking the SATs and then, after I inevitably scored lower than I did the first time, to sue my college for diseducating me. *Diseducate* isn't even a word. That's how dumb I am. Maybe more unpleasant than finding out how tragic your verbal and mathematical abilities are, however, is learning, to the exact number, how deficiently your intelligence measures up against the norm. I'm talking, of course, about taking an IQ test. For the sake of science, and to amuse you at my expense, dear reader, I have elected to take the Wechsler Adult Intelligence Scale, which is nowadays the most commonly administered IQ test. After my brain has been renovated, I will endure the trial again.

Meaningful Math

1. Not the Gift of the Magi

Jackie had a husband and a paramour and she loved them very much, but not as much as she loved the diamond brooch that caught her attention one day in the window of Van Cleef & Arpels. The jewel went for an ungodly sum, call it x, and she was not God, but no matter: As she explained to the salesclerk, she had a plan. The next day Jackie escorted her husband to the shop, where much ogling went on—she toward the brooch and he in the direction of his wife. "A treasure for a treasure," said Jackie's husband, taking out his credit card. "The clasp needs repair," said the salesclerk, "so I will give you a fifteen percent discount. You can pick it up in a week." The next day Jackie brought her paramour to the shop and did what women do with their wiles. The wiles worked. "We'll take the brooch," her paramour said to the salesclerk, "and I'll pay cash." "In that case I'll give you a ten percent discount," said the salesclerk, "but you'll have to wait a week to pick up the item because I must replace the backing." A week later Jackie had her brooch, which she wore insouciantly in the company of her husband and her paramour alike. She and the salesclerk split the profit—that is, the amount netted after the original sticker price was deducted. Each ended up with $30,000. How much did the brooch originally sell for? Hint: This requires math.

ANSWER: $80,000

2. And We're Not Even Talking About Money

The Pomegranates are remodeling their bathroom. The contractor promises that he and his assistant Drago can do the job in fifteen days. Drago works three times as fast as the contractor. On day two Drago is stricken with a hangnail and cannot work. Ever. The contractor hires Buster and Lester, who together can work one-fourth as fast as Drago worked. What Buster and Lester lack in speed, they do not make up for in carefulness. They put the toilet in upside down. The resulting flood spreads to the kitchen. The contractor says that redoing the kitchen and replacing the dog will take six times as long as the bathroom. The contractor fires Buster and Lester and employs a team whose religious habits permit them to work only on days that begin with a *T*. The first day on the job, the team works ten times as fast as the contractor. Every day thereafter it works half as fast as the day before. The Pomegranates divorce. Mrs. Pomegranate is institutionalized. Will the bathroom be painted by the time Mrs. Pomegranate gets out of the bug house?

ANSWER:

Yes, but when she sees that it is painted Crème Fraîche instead of Fraîche Crème, she will check herself back in.

3. Now We're Talking About Money

Liz Taylor has been married three times. No, not that Liz Taylor, another Liz Taylor. She received a modest settlement from each ex. The amounts, in chronological order, were as follows: $1,000, $8,000, $27,000. She put this money into a fund to pay for her twins' college education, but do you think it will cover the cost of even a semester? Her children will be attending Sarah Lawrence, the most expensive college in the country (doesn't it figure?). The tuition is $66,259, and that's just this year, and that doesn't include books, though maybe they're not necessary. Child support? There is none. It's a long story. Considering extras and assuming tuition raises, let's say Liz Taylor is going to have to cough up $600,000 over four years. How many more times must Liz Taylor get divorced?

ANSWER: 3

Which Came First?

———

DIRECTIONS:

This quiz is self-explanatory, but if you have one of those selves who is above directions, listen up.

Number each entry in chronological order, with 1 being the first or oldest. Here's an example:

__ June 3
__ June 1
__ June 2

ANSWERS:

 _3_   June 3

 _1_   June 1

 _2_   June 2

How'd you do? Now you're on your own. I'll see you at the answer key on page 101.

Eons 'n' Things

__ Iron Age

__ Bronze Age

__ *The Age of Innocence* (the movie)

__ US drinking age raised from eighteen to twenty-one

__ Art Nouveau

__ First Paleolithic diet

__ Cronuts

__ Ice Age

__ Art Deco

Makeovers

__ French Revolution

__ Industrial Revolution

__ Sexual Revolution

__ "Revolution 9" by the Beatles

__ Chanel No. 5

__ October Revolution

__ Arab Spring

__ Decembrist Revolt in the Russian Empire

Divorce, Annulment, Legal Separation, Plus Happy Rockefeller

__ Diana Spencer

__ Anne Boleyn

__ Pompeia

__ Kim Kardashian (from first husband nobody has
heard of)

__ Happy Rockefeller

__ Catherine of Aragon

__ Joséphine de Beauharnais

__ Catherine Dickens

__ Elin Nordegren

You Used to Know This

__ *The Bob Newhart Show*

__ Tiny Tim marries Miss Vicky

__ Nixon resigns

__ Hot pants hot

__ Cuban Missile Crisis (you're not thinking of the
Bay of Pigs, are you?)

__ First test tube baby born

__ Lucy gives birth to Little Ricky

You Never Knew This

__ Telephone

__ Printing press (European)

__ Bessemer steel

__ Spinning jenny

__ Pancakes

__ Repeating rifle
__ Repeating rifle
__ Hats
__ Repeating rifle

Calendar

__ Arbor Day in the United States
__ Presidents' Day
__ No Pants Day
__ Halloween
__ Jewish Halloween
__ Thanksgiving
__ Bastille Day
__ Gay Purim
__ Earth Day

Candyland

__ Blueberry
__ Cherry
__ Grape (real)
__ Tangerine
__ Grape (artificial)
__ Yellow

___ Rasapple (raspberry + apple)
___ Pimento
___ Blood

Protein

___ Chicken
___ Egg

ANSWERS:

Eons 'n' Things

__1__ Ice Age

__2__ First Paleolithic diet

__3__ Bronze Age

__4__ Iron Age

__5__ Art Nouveau

__6__ Art Deco

__7__ *The Age of Innocence* (the movie)

__8__ US drinking age raised from eighteen to twenty-one

__9__ Cronuts

Makeovers

 1   Decembrist Revolt in the Russian
     Empire

 2   French Revolution

 3   Industrial Revolution

 4   October Revolution

 5   "Revolution 9" by the Beatles

 6   Sexual Revolution

 7   Chanel No. 5

 8   Arab Spring

*Divorce, Annulment, Legal Separation,
Plus Happy Rockefeller*

 1   Pompeia

 2   Catherine of Aragon

 3   Anne Boleyn

 4   Joséphine de Beauharnais

 5   Catherine Dickens

 6   Happy Rockefeller

 7   Diana Spencer

_8_ Elin Nordegren

_9_ Kim Kardashian (from first husband nobody has heard of)

You Used to Know This

_1_ Lucy gives birth to Little Ricky

_2_ Cuban Missile Crisis

_3_ Hot pants hot

_4_ Tiny Tim marries Miss Vicky

_5_ *The Bob Newhart Show*

_6_ Nixon resigns

_7_ First test tube baby born

You Never Knew This

_1_ Hats [older]

_2_ Pancakes [old]

_3_ Printing press (European) [1450]

_4_ Spinning jenny [1764]

_5_ Bessemer steel [1855]

_6_ Repeating rifle [1860s]

_6_ Repeating rifle [1860s]

_6_ Repeating rifle [1860s]

_7_ Telephone [1876]

Calendar

_1_ No Pants Day

_2_ Presidents' Day

_3_ Jewish Halloween

_4_ Earth Day

_5_ Arbor Day

_6_ Gay Purim

_7_ Bastille Day

_8_ Halloween

_9_ Thanksgiving

Candyland

Note: This one is alphabetical.

_1_ Blood

_2_ Blueberry

_3_ Cherry

_4_ Grape (artificial)

_5_ Grape (real)

_6_ Pimento

_7_ Rasapple (raspberry + apple)

_8_ Tangerine

_9_ Yellow

Protein

_1_ Chicken

_2_ Egg

Note: In 2010, scientists determined that the chicken came before the egg. Anyone who answered before 2010 gets credit if you got it wrong.

SCORING:

To figure out your score start out at 64. Deduct 1 for each entry you got wrong. Now deduct 1 for each Google search. And now subtract another 2 for each time Google autocorrected your spelling. Compare your scores below.

65–56: Herodotus

You know all of history! Even the part that doesn't repeat itself.

55–45: Adjunct History Professor

You know a lot about history. Not enough for tenure, obviously, but enough to be comfortable.

44–35: Potter

You are more disposed toward clay and a knack for glazed mugs.

34–25: *Homo erectus*

That Herodotus thing earlier went right over your head.

24–15: Know-Nothing

You got defensive when you saw *Homo erectus* a second ago. That's not what it means, though, and you're overreacting.

14–5: Homeschooled for Political Reasons

Really? Some of this stuff you should just know for daily chores. How do you pay taxes or buy groceries?

4–1: Jellyfish

You are a jellyfish! A gelatinous member of the Cnidaria phylum employing propulsion for movement. You do not even have vision or nerves. What are you doing taking this quiz, jellyfish?

0– –10: Alien being

You scare me. Go away.

IQ tests are meant to assess not how much you know (phew) but how inherently bright you are (uh-oh). This type of aptitude, called *fluid intelligence*, is based on your facility for reasoning abstractly, solving problems in novel situations, and remembering to bring a sharpened number two pencil. Some neuropsychologists would also add to the list motivation to score well. The other kind of smarts, the kind that IQ tests do not care about, is called *crystallized intelligence*. This sort of intelligence, which tends to expand as we age, comes from learning and experience. Knowing the meaning of the term *crystallized intelligence* is an example of crystallized intelligence.

The good thing—or wait, is it the bad thing?—about taking an IQ test is that unlike with, say, trying to ace the *Jeopardy!* Daily Double or pass your driver's test, studying will get you nowhere. Your cognitive capacity, say many researchers, is largely, though not entirely, determined early. If you'd only been thinking before you were born, you might have chosen different parents—from 40 to 80 percent of your intelligence is inherited. It's not too late, however, to blame the mother and father you ended up with for raising you on Doritos, Velveeta, and Mountain Dew. Children, particularly males, who were breastfed until they were six months old and who dined on healthy foods as toddlers seem to have marginally higher IQs (as much as two points) at age eight.

Is it possible after the age of three to hike up your IQ? When I was a kid, one's IQ was top secret—a

God-given barometer of consequence that was known only to the authorities and inscribed on your Permanent Record. A few of my classmates claimed to have discovered their IQs—and guess what? Every one of them was genius material. (By the way, 140 is the cutoff for genius, but 160, reputed to be the IQ of Einstein, will qualify you to be a genius genius.) The rest of us worried that we were destined to be enduringly dumb, for back then, the conventional wisdom about wisdom was that your IQ was immutable—like your hair color (little did I know!). Today most scientists, though not all, believe that by regularly challenging yourself with a variety of novel and complex mental activities, and by living a drab life (exercise, meditation, ground flaxseed, etc.), it is possible to increase your IQ or at least improve your test-taking skills, if not your intelligence. Whether IQ is indeed a true measure of thinking ability and neural efficiency has stumped greater minds than mine. Bear this in mind, though: Cartoon celebrity Lisa Simpson has an IQ of 156, one point higher than the Rembrandts and Jonathan Swifts. I rest my case. Oh, wait—I unrest my case so that I can present one more item: My microwave is a Genius. I'm not bragging—that is Panasonic's name for it, and anyway, yesterday it broke. I am replacing it with an LG LMH2016, which is probably a moron.

Another way to raise your IQ is to be born in the future. According to data collected since the test has been documented, the average IQ around the world has been increasing by about three points every decade, a phenomenon called the Flynn effect. Nobody knows for sure why this is so, though theories abound— healthier diets, more widespread schooling, greater familiarity with tests, smaller families, earlier maturation of children, etc. The explanation that James Flynn favors—and after all, it's his effect—posits that society nowadays encourages more abstract problem-solving than in the past; to a great extent, this is the very facility that IQ tests measure. Take, for instance, the word similarities sub-test on the Wechsler Intelligence Scale. Flynn gives this example to demonstrate how our thought processes have changed over the years. To the question "What do dogs and rabbits have in common?" most respondents today would answer (correctly) that they are both mammals. Someone who lives in a less complicated world, however, might answer: "We use dogs to hunt for rabbits." "The right answer," Flynn writes in *Are We Getting Smarter?: Rising IQ in the Twenty-First Century,* "assumes that you are conditioned to look at the world in a certain way: through scientific spectacles—as something to be understood by classification; and not through utilitarian spectacles—as something to be manipulated to advantage." Um, maybe. Still, don't you think that second guy is a little stupid?

In any case, cramming for the Wechsler the night before will not give you an IQ higher than your cholesterol. But how could I resist? As a rehearsal for my psychometric ordeal, I decided to take my neurons on some trial runs by sampling several free online IQ tests. By *free* I mean that they cost money—not the tests per se, but the results (anywhere from $9.95 to fifty dollars, sometimes with bonus personality test included). A handful of outfits online offer the kit and caboodle without charge—and I completed as many of those questionnaires as I could tolerate. The items range from simple analogies (head is to hat as hand is to glove) to spatial puzzles that invite you to imagine reconstructing deconstructed polyhedra and then rotating them in order to determine which plane ends up next to which other plane, a task that makes my brain stand up and scream.

Please, whatever you do, don't make me tell you again how I scored. If you'd like to revisit my humiliation, see the second page of the prologue.

The first time I was evaluated by a psychologist, I was about six. My parents were concerned because I still wet my bed. The psychologist watched me play with blocks and showed me some inkblots. He came to a conclusion: "In my judgment," my parents say he said, "your daughter is lazy and will never get into a good college."

This time an affable young woman in charge of psychological assessment at NYU School of Medicine at Bellevue Hospital would superintend. The process, she warned me in an e-mail, could last five hours. "Try not to worry too much," she wrote after I sent her a worried note. "We will make it fun!" This made me more worried.

It was a four-hour undertaking, and not as agonizing as I'd expected, but what is? I wish I could disclose the test questions, but because the Wechsler Adult Intelligence Scale is copyright-protected, it was requested that I not reveal this information. Also, letting you in on what to expect would thereafter skew the average IQ upward, which would make me seem even more dim-witted (is it possible to have a negative IQ?), and that is something I need like a hole in my head. Another reason I can't divulge the exact questions is that I forget what they are.

As long as you don't tell on me I guess I won't get in too much trouble by advising you to bone up on your block design. Also, it wouldn't hurt to practice repeating series of numbers in reverse order—but you probably already do that. There's also a mathematical game that looks like a Fisher-Price toy for eighteen-month-olds and involves strategically moving doughnut-shaped disks from one peg to another. In addition to these sorts of merriments, there is a seven-page personality test consisting of statements, a few of them startlingly kooky, to which one must respond (1) very true, (2) true, (3) somewhat true, (4) not very true, or (5) false. If you answer "very true" to the statement "Most people look forward to a trip to the dentist," it means you are (1) high on nitrous oxide, (2) a dentist with a child in college, or (3) deliberately trying to foil the results. (The answer is 3, and this is typical of the sort of question planted in the IQ test to make sure you're not answering honestly and to the best of your ability. So watch it.)

My apologies for this chapter's anticlimax, but, just as I chose not to find out the results of my brain scans until undergoing the follow-up test, I will, no matter what my editor says, put off knowing my score as long as possible, or at least until my brain is wised up. In the meantime you might be interested to know that just now, when I took an online quiz in order to find out "what your name should be," I was informed, "Tiffany is the best name for you. You're charming and you rock those heels, girl!"

WHICH BANANA IS THE RIPEST?

Wishes he were
a nectarine

Is afraid of
being eaten

Grew up on a
bottom branch

Answers to name
of Butch

Spent last week in a bag with a
tomato doing god knows what

Has a dirty
mind

Hates her
neck

Consulted with a
dermatologist about
her spots

Once fell on floor

Brown spots in
formation of the
Leeward Islands

Suffers from
a Napoleonic
complex

Great-great-great-
great-etc.
grandson of
banana on
Warhol's Velvet
Underground
album cover

ANSWER:

Ethylene gas is what causes a banana to ripen. Bananas produce their own ethylene, but adding more causes them to ripen faster. Thus, after shipment, green bananas are often gassed with ethylene. Tomatoes, apples, and pears produce the hydrocarbon, which is why putting bananas in a bag with any of these fruits accelerates the ripening process. Thus the banana that hung out with the tomato is the ripest.

Killer Quiz

It's time to test your assassination literacy. If you can't figure out the directions to this quiz, deduct twenty-five points from your IQ.

ASSASSINATEE	ASSASSINATOR
Julius Caesar	*(Two answers accepted)*
	Charlotte Corday
	Gavrilo Princip
	Ramón Mercader
Lee Harvey Oswald	
Robert F. Kennedy	
Martin Luther King	*(Alleged; two answers accepted)*
John Lennon	
	Dan White
	Kristin Shepard (played by Mary Crosby)

Bonus question: Who didn't kill Gerald Ford?

ANSWERS:

ASSASSINATEE	ASSASSINATOR
Julius Caesar	Marcus Junius Brutus, Gaius Cassius Longinus
Jean-Paul Marat	Charlotte Corday
Archduke Franz Ferdinand	Gavrilo Princip
Leon Trotsky	Ramón Mercader
Lee Harvey Oswald	Jack Ruby
Robert F. Kennedy	Sirhan Sirhan
Martin Luther King	Thought to be James Earl Ray or Loyd Jowers
John Lennon	Mark David Chapman
Harvey Milk	Dan White
J.R.	Kristin Shepard (played by Mary Crosby)

ANSWER TO BONUS QUESTION:

Lynette "Squeaky" Fromme

Chapter Six

My Brain Goes to Gym Class (But at Least It Doesn't Have to Play Dodgeball)

Do I seem smarter than I did in chapter five? Since then I've spent untellable hours in front of my computer, challenged by earth-shattering problems like which tiles on the matrix were momentarily highlighted, how to maneuver a penguin through a constantly rotating maze, and how many more drills I must complete before I am smart enough to date Harold Bloom. If it were not for these distractions, dumb ol' me could have finished writing chapter eleven by now.

Remember when video games were considered the pastimes of sketchy children, whose addiction, if left unchecked, could lead to a life of crime and poor eye-sight? Now we call these games *brain exercises* and hope and trust that our digital exertions will make us as mentally agile as preteens wielding M27 assault rifles in Call of Duty: Black Ops II. They—the games, not the guns—are to mental health what kale and juice cleanses are to nutrition.

"Improve your brain performance," beckons one online cognitive training website, "and live a better life." "Achieve up to 1500% increase in brain func-tion," is the come-on from a "learning enhancement" outfit. Let's be honest: Wouldn't it be great if I could prescribe a regimen of computer workouts I'd devised and guarantee that if you played them ten minutes a day, you'd never ever have any mental boo-boos as long as you live and that you'd always remember the name of that lady you keep running into on the elevator? With more baby boomers reported to be afraid of los-ing their minds than of dying, the worried well—and also a few who aren't doing so hot—spend more than a billion dollars a year on brain fitness. I'd be so rich! Er, what I mean is that helping others turn back their cognitive clocks would bring me immense joy.

Do these programs really work? Define *work*. Never mind. Nobody can agree on that anyway. What is beyond arguing about is that these games make you better at these games. Keep practicing Leap Froggies, and sooner or later you will become a pro at getting all the brown frogs to the rocks on the right side of the screen and all the green frogs to the rocks on the left side. OK, but what if your ambitions are loftier than successfully regrouping a bunch of animated amphibians? Will becoming super-duper at playing computer games translate to sharper overall cognitive performance? Will it enable you to differentiate Emma Watson from Emma Stone from Emma Roberts from Emma Woodhouse? Help you remember where you parked the car? Help you remember you don't own a car? Provide you with the mental capacity to understand why there is more matter than antimatter in the observable universe? (See me if you know the answer. We can share the Nobel.) Moreover, will those benefits be long-lasting? Such is the hallowed mission of all brain game designers. You can answer either yes or no to these questions, and either way you will be in the company of reputable scientists.

There are studies that conclude exercising your brain makes you a more logical problem-solver and more capable multitasker, improves your short-term memory, boosts your IQ, delays mental decline by ten years, lowers your risk of an automobile crash, revs up skills that would make you a more reliable air traffic controller, tunes up your motor coordination so that you can perform laparoscopic surgery optimally, helps you manage physical pain, and makes you happier—and also sexier. (Not really about that last one.) Controlled studies have shown that after just ten hours of cognitive conditioning, gains can persist for as long as ten years. I have also read studies—and meta-studies—that dispute each of these studies, followed by critiques of those critiques.

One of the most influential studies (and one that has been both proven and disproven too many times for my little hippocampus to keep track of) was done in 2008 by Susanne Jaeggi and Martin Buschkuehl, who demonstrated that playing a certain memory game enhanced the player's intelligence. The game in question was based on the n-*back task*. Subjects were shown a sequence of rapidly changing screens on which a blue square appeared in various positions. At the same time, a series of letters was recited to the group. The subjects were then asked whether the screen and/or letter matched the corresponding items from two cycles ago. Depending on the subject's performance as the game progressed, the number of cycles he or she was asked to remember increased or decreased—hence the *n* in *n*-back. And you thought charades was hard to follow. Doesn't this game sound like a barrel of laughs? Fun or otherwise, the longer the subjects played, claimed Jaeggi and Buschkuehl, the better they scored on tests that measured general intelligence.

A few years earlier, a researcher in Sweden, Torkel Klingberg, showed that children with attention deficit/ hyperactivity disorder (ADHD) could become smarter if they played memory-augmenting computer games. I am mentioning Torkel Klingberg here because I love his name. Also, as you will see if you consult Google Images, he is very cute.

It was partly as a result of the n-back findings that many scientists started to believe that the wrinkly guck inside our skulls might be trainable. Given that supposition, we were a mere metaphor away from the proposal that we can have hunky brains if we just do a few exercises—not unlike the way you lift weights and do abdominal crunches to stay as buff and adorable as ever. This is not an unreasonable theory.

How come you can't just do crosswords? To everyone who has solved today's puzzle: Sorry, but this is no guarantee you will end up less nutty than the rest of us. Says Alvaro Fernandez, CEO of SharpBrains (the market research firm concerned with brain health, in case you've forgotten), "Once someone has done hundreds or thousands of puzzles, the marginal benefit tends toward zero because it becomes just another routine, easy activity—probably a bit more stimulating and effortful than watching TV, but not enough to bring benefits other than becoming a master at crossword puzzles." If you're practiced enough to know that *auk* is a diving seabird, it's time to learn sign language or take up the tuba. The key to staying sharp, says Fernandez, is to challenge your brain continually with a variety of novel activities—in other words, become a serious dilettante.

CROSSWORD PUZZLE
of
CROSSWORDIEST WORDS*

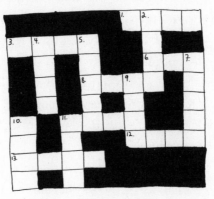

* Words with highest ratio of appearances in The New York Times crossword puzzle to appearances in books scanned by google. From a list compiled by Noah Veltman (who is a "web developer").

Clues:

ACROSS:

1. Hey, you!

3. Up in the sky, look: It's a bird! It's a plane! No, it's a bear.

6. Approximately when I'll get there

8. The side of the ship you want to be on if you don't want your hair to get messed up

11. You should have bought an apartment here a long time ago when all the artists lived here. Now you can't afford even a latte in this district.

12. Ew! Gross! What happened to your eye? (And why are you spelling the disease with an *e* at the end?)

13. Where you are when you're puking from all that rolling, pitching, and yawing

DOWN:

2. A dagger from Ye Olden Days. One letter different from another word you don't know (11 down).

4. Goddess whose children were swallowed by Cronus, who was her brother and husband. Awkward!

5. No matter how bad your memory is, this is something to remember

7. Nest for eagles who don't have a fear of heights

9. Son of Seth; grandson of Adam. What, you don't read the Bible? Then: *The Dukes of Hazzard* spin-off.

10. Holy moly!

11. Pirate in Peter Pan (see 2 down, if you feel like it)

ANSWERS:

1. P 2. S S T
3. U 4. R S 5. A / N
H / L / 6. E T / 7. A
E / 8. A L 9. E E / E
A / M / N / R
10. E / 11. S O H O / I
G / M / 12. S T Y E
13. A S E A
D / E

Instead of games, then, why not invigorate your brain by playing bridge, becoming a chess master, curing a disease, or untangling your earphone cords? Because: Isn't it easier just to pay $9.95 a month and push some buttons on the electronic device of your choice?

Yes.

Enter the entrepreneurs. Within the last few years, enough brain fitness products have been developed by neuroscience companies to give each of your synapses its very own personal training program. Here is a partial list of companies and programs: MindSparke, MyBrainSolutions, Brain Spa, brainTivity, Brainiversity,

Brain Metrix, BrainHQ, Mind Quiz: Your Brain Coach, Brain Exercise with Dr. Kawashima, Nintendo's Brain Age, Advanced Brain Technologies, Cogmed, Lumosity, MindHabits, NeuroNation, and HAPPYneuron. I predict that as long as there is a thesaurus, this list will grow.

By far the biggest purveyor in the field is Lumos Labs, the neuroscience research company that sells the Lumosity training program. As of April 2015, this brain trust, which has grown 200 percent every year since the launch of its software in 2007, had sixty million subscribers in at least 180 countries. This is about the same as the population of Italy.

One of the subscribers is me. Another is Teresa Heinz Kerry, wife of Secretary of State John Kerry, who began using Lumosity on her iPad after she had a stroke and credits the program with accelerating her recovery, but this isn't a self-help book for Theresa. Every day I, Patty, am presented with five games in my in-box.

This is the part where I should probably describe how to play all of these games, but that would be as peppy to read as the booklet on how to care for your new washer/dryer unit. Suffice it to say, each task seems to have been specially tailored to make me feel bad about a specific mental faculty (memory, attention, speed of processing, flexibility, or problem-solving, depending on the game). Moreover, most of the challenges are timed, and so, as the clock ticks, my heart pounds like a Gene Krupa solo. I am especially undone by the game Raindrops, which calls on the player to solve equations that reside inside descending raindrops before those numeral-filled drips reach the ocean. Under this kind of pressure, can anyone be expected to add even 1 + 1? (Brain scans of subjects who are afraid of math show that the mere thought of having to do math triggered responses in the subject that looked just like the images of someone experiencing physical pain.) Also nerve-destroying is Brain Shift, which requires one to, ever so speedily, press the right arrow key when the number is even or the letter is a vowel, and the left arrow key when the number is odd or the letter is a consonant. This doesn't sound hard but, believe me, people have telephoned 911 for less.

According to the Lumosity website, in the past 103 days, I have played 876 games. I know what you're thinking: "5 × 103 does not = 876. No wonder she is having trouble with simple arithmetic." You are probably also thinking, "Is she on steroids?" Or, if you are my mother, you are thinking—actually, saying, "You're sure you're not doing too many exercises? What if something in your head snaps?" Here's the thing: The reason my count is this ridiculously high is that so determined am I to have an enviable LPI (Lumosity Performance

Index) that I play each game not just once but repeatedly. Feel free to substitute the word *repeatedly* with *until the cows come home*. A session is supposed to last about ten minutes. Mine can last up to two hours. Lumosity recommends three to five workouts a week. I never miss a day. Now you are really starting to wonder about me, aren't you? Maybe I shouldn't tell you, then, that in addition to those completed games I've chalked up, I've started many others and then, sensing that things were not going well, thrown in the towel and pressed restart, blaming my bad performance on my computer or on hearing my boyfriend breathe in the next room or, though we haven't met, sometimes even on you, who I so don't want to disappoint. The next game, I tell myself, will be perfect. Is this cheating? Sort of, I guess. Pathetic? You bet!

LPI is like the Dow-Jones average of your brain. The number goes up or down daily, depending on your performance that day—as well as on previous days. The index is based on an algorithm that takes into account the scores of millions of players. Thus you can not only feel bad by comparing your today self against yesterday self, you can also feel bad by lining up against those in your age group or any other age group you choose. This is the only advantage to getting old I can think of—that your Lumosity competition is not as stiff. Tip:

Whatever you do, don't compare yourself against the twenty- to twenty-four-year-olds. They are the worst, by which I mean the best.

As anyone would predict, my LPI increased over time.

MY PROGRESS

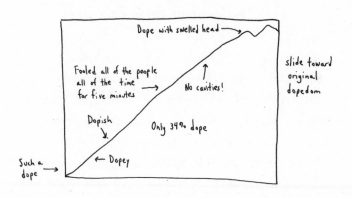

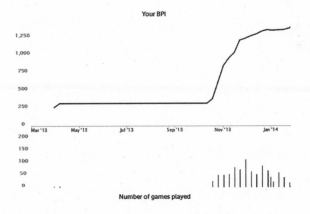

Do these scores translate to increased intelligence in my so-called real life? I guess we'll find out soon. In the meantime, isn't it curious that on one of my absolute highest-performing days, as I was setting up the Lumosity app on my phone, I forgot my password?

Are You Smarter Yet? (Part One)

Is this book doing its job? Here's a diagnostic crossword to help you find out if you are less stupid than you were on page one. Don't be discouraged if you can't complete this puzzle within two hours. If you're stuck, give me a call, and I'll provide a hint. Ready? Don't be afraid to answer

YES.

ARE YOU SMARTER YET?
(PART 1)

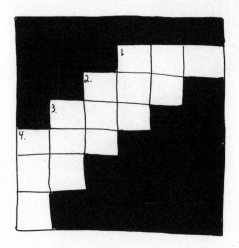

CLUES

Across

1. Opposite of "no"
2. "Oui" in English
3. An affirmative
4. See 2 down

Down

1. "S-E-Y" backwards
2. Acronym for Young Elderly Society
3. Formal for "yeah"
4. Synonym for "yes"

ANSWERS:

Paradox at the Greek Diner

Late one night Frank stops at a Greek diner that has only two waiters, Nick and Zorba. One always tells the truth, and the other always lies. Which is which is unclear. I know, I know—this is a bad business model, but can I get on with my paradox? To wash down his baklava, Frank orders a cup of decaf from Zorba. "You're sure it's decaf?" says a nervous Frank to Zorba as the waiter pours him some coffee. "I always tell the truth," says Zorba. Nick appears at the table with another pot of coffee, which he insists is decaf. "Don't believe Zorba," says Nick. "He's a liar." "Nick's a liar," says Zorba. "Zorba's the liar," says Nick. This witty badinage continues, but we don't have to bear witness. What's important is that only one of the pots of coffee is indeed decaf. Is it, then, Zorba or Nick who is telling the truth? Are there any question(s) Frank can ask to find out? Or should he just order tea?

ANSWER:

Frank can uncover the truth by asking just one question. In fact, two different questions will each provide all the enlightenment he needs, coffee-wise.

1. "If I ask the other waiter whether your coffee is decaf, will he answer yes or no?"

   If Frank asks Zorba this question, and Zorba is the truth-teller, then Zorba will say that Nick, the liar, will say that no, Zorba's coffee is not decaffeinated. If Zorba is a liar, then he will say that Nick will say yes, Zorba's coffee is decaf. If Frank asks Nick this same question, the same logic applies. Thus no means yes and vice versa.

2. "What would your answer be if I asked you if
   your coffee was decaf?"
      If Zorba is the truth-teller, he will say yes
   if his coffee is decaf, and no if it isn't. If he
   is the liar and his coffee is decaf, he will lie
   about his lie and say no if his coffee is decaf
   and yes if his coffee is not decaf. Thus, in this
   hypothetical, yes means yes and no means no.

You are on your own with figuring out the tip.

Chapter Seven

Pole-Vaulting My Way to Intellectual Heights. I Mean Stepping on a Kitchen Chair to Reach the Low-Fat Mayonnaise.

As someone whose favorite sport is sitting, I would just once like to hear some bad news about physical exercise. Why can't researchers discover that lunges cause a decline in SAT scores or that spinning class makes you so addled you forget how to use a semicolon? Regrettably, you will hear nothing of the sort if you talk to neurologists. They will tell you that whether you are young or old, aerobic exertion—even a schlumpy amount—increases the number of blood vessels carrying oxygen to your upper level. They will say that tiring activities spur the growth of neurons and trigger the formation of a class of proteins that stimulate the growth of axons, enabling your brain cells to reach out and touch one another, thus expanding your circuitry up there. As if there were not already enough reasons to work out, neurologists, armed with clinical trials and studies, have added "better thinking" to the list.

I sought an exercise routine that was suited to my strengths and schedule. No, not darts. Every day—dutifully, resentfully, tediously, miserably, and always without the slightest hint of an endorphin to cheer me along—I engaged in a high-intensity circuit training program comprised of twelve exercises, such as tricep dips (on the chair) and push-ups with side rotation (too boring to explain). The drill was developed by the Human Performance Institute and recommended by the *New York Times*. In total, including the rests between the exercises, it lasts seven minutes.

There is only one thing more boring than exercising. That is reading about exercising. Let us move on to the next paragraph because it is a hopeful one.

Scientists are developing a pill that may mimic the beneficial cognitive effects of exercise. Essentially, the pill contains a hormone (FNDC5) that prods the expression of BDNF and other neurotrophic factors, which in turn activate genes involved in learning and memory. Now that is something to sit down and shout hooray about.

This just in: Researchers in Norway have come up with the four-minute workout.

EXTREME
EXERCISES

LEG LIFTS

WHAT COMES NEXT?

1. 2. 3. 4.

You will have to flip to page 138 for the answers. This counts as exercise.

YOGA POSES

WHAT COMES NEXT?

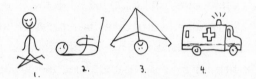

1.   2.   3.   4.

WEIGHTS

1 lb.   4 lb.   27 lb.   256 lb.

WHAT COMES NEXT?

256 lb.   562 lb.   3125 lb.   632845 lb.

1.   2.   3.   4.

ANSWERS: 2, 4, 3

May I interrupt myself here and say that the way you've been turning the pages lately shows uncanny astuteness? Let's see how smart you've become.

ARE YOU SMARTER YET?

(PART 2)

This psychological test is designed to evaluate your planning, reasoning, and problem-solving skills as well as your ability to find a pencil. This maze could also be helpful in gauging your spatial learning and memory, especially if you are a rodent.

DIRECTIONS:

Trace a path from the mouse to the cheese. Try to avoid dead ends. No backtracking is permitted. You have seven days to complete the test.

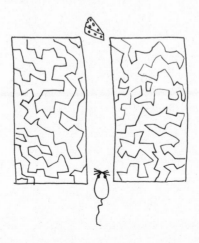

Chapter Eight

Om, Um, Oy

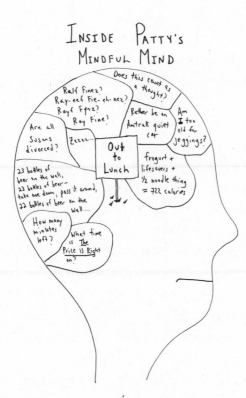

INSIDE PATTY'S
MINDFUL MIND

Does this count as a thought?

Ralf Finez?
Ray-eef Fie-eh-nez?
Rayf Fynz?
Ray Fine?

Rather be on Amtrak quiet car

Am I too old for jeggings?

Are all Susans divorced?

Zzzzz...

Out to Lunch

frogurt + lifesavers + ½ noodle thing = 722 calories

23 bottles of beer on the wall, 23 bottles of beer— take one down, pass it around, 22 bottles of beer on the wall...

How many minutes left?

What time is _The Price is Right_ on?

During my hitchhiking days—that would be in the 1970s, when I was in college—I was picked up by a free spirit in a VW Beetle. She wore beads and a dress seemingly made out of an old Indian bedspread or an old Indian. Handing me a piece of paper printed with the words *Nam Myoh Renge Kyo*, she promised that if I chanted the phrase a few times a day, I'd be granted happiness or whatever. Don't say I didn't try. I was sick of hitchhiking. I wanted a car. To this day I have never owned a car. (I no longer want one, so maybe that's how the magic works.)

Years later I met a man at a party who explained why he meditated: "You know how when you're born into the world, you're pure love and essence, but it gets covered by your personality so you're not living? Meditation realigns you with the universe. I also do a lot of spiritual work, such as past-life regressions. I try to live in the present in the presence."

I know I know I know: It is unenlightened of me to let these encounters prejudice my view of meditation—or to equate the discipline with daydreaming, napping, yoga pants, or Seinfeld's show about nothing. Sixty-seven percent of Americans ruminate and reflect for at least thirty minutes a week. I made this figure up, but sometimes you just have to do the right thing. Don't all your friends, and not just the dumb ones, swear to you that meditation has transformed their lives, made them more productive, less agitated, and kinder—as well as better skiers.

Lately scientists have become very rah-rah about meditation. The claim is that it makes gray matter denser in the hippocampus (camping grounds for memory and learning) and less dense in the amygdala (anxiety and stress). Training a mere twenty minutes a day for four days supposedly can make you remarkably better at processing information and sustaining attention. In other words, it raises your IQ in less time than I spend deciding what to wear. Meditation can supposedly even treat attention deficit disorders.

They also say it works wonders on your immune system, lowers your blood pressure, and makes you more altruistic and less likely to become obese, but that is a different book, not this book. Let's return to what those scientists said about attention.

I could use some buckling down. My mental skyscape has too many aircraft aloft.

There are more techniques for elevating your state of consciousness than there are Heinz varieties. You can do it with or without a mantra, sitting up straight or lying down (it's called bed med and I didn't make that up), allowing your mind to wander freely as if it were a Montessori school student or reining your thoughts in as if they were citizens of North Korea. Among the odder types of meditation are labyrinth (walking through a maze as a way to spark creativity and problem-solving), laughter (giggles supposedly boost soothing hormones while lessening stress-inducing ones), and fire (staring at a flame can create a trance; not to be confused with arson meditation).

After some meditation on meditation, I chose the kind called *mindfulness* because feeling a little mindless, I thought I could use some more mind.

Jon Kabat-Zinn, a molecular biologist turned secular god in the mindfulness movement defines the approach as "paying attention, in a particular way, on purpose, in the present moment, and nonjudgmentally." A friend said, "It's about treating your thoughts like sheep. They come in, you herd them out. The more you practice the stronger your anti-ADD muscle becomes." Although Buddhist-inspired, the technique is secular enough that the US military dabbles in it. I could have signed up for a Transcendental Meditation course but that costs around $1,500. (Participants are sworn not to divulge what they learn, but I found out; I can't tell you how—e-mail if you want to know.)

I clicked on a cosmos of instructional videos on YouTube that featured vistas of fluffy clouds, waves breaking on the beach, sunsets, and any number of other pictures that look like the photographs you've removed from store-bought frames, and as I listened to earnest disembodied voices intone about how sublimely relaxed I was feeling, I couldn't resist the urge to buy under-eye concealer on Amazon. Later, with a hundred or more others, I took an introductory meditation class at the Tibet House in Manhattan, and while everyone else was presumably letting the sounds wash through them, bringing their attention to the sensation of their bodies sitting, and not judging themselves, I spent my time wishing everyone would put their shoes back on. During the Q&A portion, a woman asked the teacher, "My dogs crawl all over me when I meditate. What should I do?" Teacher: "I don't know. I don't have that problem." Finally a friend and I took a series of four one-hour private lessons with a student of Kabat-Zinn who talked a lot about her personal journey and then led us in a raisin consciousness exercise in which we were encouraged to explore a single raisin using all our senses. "If you understand the raisin," said our teacher, "you understand mindfulness." That's a big if.

Achieving inner calm may be the simplest thing I cannot do—that, and making coffee. The instructions regarding the former are straightforward: (1) Sit down. (2) Close your eyes or, if you don't feel like it, keep them open. (3) Pay attention to your breathing—the way it feels in your nose, lungs, etc. (4) When your mind forgets to pay attention to your breathing, and trust me, it will, take note of where your mind goes but don't be high-handed about it. It's only a mind, after all. (5) Return to the tedium of keeping track of your breathing. (6) Do this for the rest of your life.

I did everything I was told, but to no avail. Again I am reminded of the 1970s, which were my days not only of hitchhiking, but also of limited drug sampling. "Do you feel it yet?" a friend who was feeling it would say after we'd both ingested something that was supposed to be mind-altering. "Not one bit," I'd say. It could be argued that I did not give meditation my all—or for that matter, my any. Perhaps this is because living with contentment and reduced anxiety doesn't seem natural. Awareness doesn't do it for me, either.

Mantra or Indian Bread

Which is which? A feature of many but not all forms of meditation, one of these is a sound you repeat silently in order to achieve a state of boredom (but in a good way). The other you eat too much of. You think you know the difference, but let's see.

1. Keema naan
2. Hum Dum Har Har
3. Aloo kulcha
4. Bhakri
5. Ram Nam
6. Pesarattu
7. Khakra
8. Thalipeeth
9. Mrityormooksheya
10. Shiam
11. Baati
12. Shreem
13. Em
14. Sheermal
15. Shring
16. Ham-Sah
17. Tat Tvam Asi
18. Aloo paratha
19. Aum
20. Uttapam
21. So ham

22. Sev puri

23. Hirim

24. Bhatoora

25. Hong-Sau

26. Benne dose

27. Pumpernickel

ANSWERS:

1. Keema naan: bread

2. Hum Dum Har Har: mantra

3. Aloo kulcha: bread

4. Bhakri: bread

5. Ram Nam: mantra

6. Pesarattu: bread

7. Khakra: bread

8. Thalipeeth: bread

9. Mrityormooksheya: mantra

10. Shiam: mantra

11. Baati: bread

12. Shreem: mantra

13. Em: mantra

14. Sheermal: bread

15. Shring: mantra

16. Ham-Sah: mantra

17. Tat Tvam Asi: mantra

18. Aloo paratha: bread

19. Aum: mantra

20. Uttapam: bread

21. So ham: mantra

22. Sev puri: bread

23. Hirim: mantra

24. Bhatoora: bread

25. Hong-Sau: mantra

26. Benne dose: bread

27. Pumpernickel: bread

YOUR SPIRITUAL QUOTIENT:

0–5: Remind me never to hire you as a waitress at the Taj Mahal Luncheonette.

10–27: You have transcended the worldly realm. Can I borrow a double sawbuck?

Perfect score: You are like the Buddha—at peace and fat.

Chapter Nine

Let's Learn Cherokee!

The only time I feel that I have a fighting chance while speaking French is when I am in a non-France foreign country. Hearing all those non-English words, my brain snaps into action. "Default to foreign language," it commands and presto, I am jabbering French to people who do not necessarily speak French. *"Très bien,"* I say, and *"Ou est le Métro?"* Otherwise, in France and for that matter in America, my French just isn't French. The last time I tried to use it in public, I was in Paris. I'd left the book I'd been reading (Kafka's letters to his girlfriend) in a movie theater and, returning the next day, put on my most mincing accent and asked the mademoiselle at the ticket booth, *"Avez-vous ma liberté?"* For those of you who know even less French than I do—if such a person exists—their word for book is *livre*.

Let's say English was not my first and second language. Let's say I mastered another language. Could bilingualism be pernicious to my mental health? Oh, come on: It doesn't really seem like such an unreasonable theory, does it? Couldn't your neurons become all balled up if you keep switching languages, in the same way that constant travel can make you confused about where you are when you wake up in the morning?

The answer is no. In fact, the answer, pardon my French, is *au contraire*. The going theory goes that because bilinguals are constantly switching between languages #1 and #2, they become practiced at attending to two tasks in rapid succession, resolving internal conflict, thinking more analytically, and keeping track of a lot of information. This rigor might explain why bilingual preschoolers performed better than their monolingual peers on a test that challenged them to sort blue circles and red shapes into (digital) bins according to shape and not color—or why babies from bilingual families did better than those from monolingual families on an exercise in which they were first trained to associate the appearance of a puppet on one half of the computer screen with an audio cue, and then retrained to look for the puppet on the other side of the screen despite the misleading audio cue.

Good for them, but is better puppet-watching skill any reason to learn another language? Here's a more persuasive argument: The average age of dementia among bilinguals is 75.5 compared to 71.4 for monolinguals.

Seventy-one point four?! My God, I could be that age one day!

I decided to learn Cherokee using the online flash cards provided on Memrise, a free website that teaches memorization through crowdsourced mnemonics. Though mostly a language-training tool, Memrise can help you become a show-off in subjects ranging from hobo symbols to famous robots, pasta shapes to Austrian army ranks, medicine to trees of England. All that is required is spending a few minutes a day for several weeks absorbing and reviewing driblets of trivia. This technique of *spaced repetition*—i.e., learning new information in short spurts and then going over it again later and still later again—is a proven method for retaining memorized material.

Why Cherokee? Because I thought it would be easy and because I was confusing it with Navajo. (Navajo

was the basis of a code Americans used during World
War Two to foil the Japanese. Cherokee also played its
part in the war, but to a far lesser extent.) Today the
Cherokee language is spoken by tribes in North Caro-
lina and Oklahoma, and by me. Correction: I have
never uttered a single Cherokee word. So far it hasn't
come up even once in conversation. This is fortunate
because I would not know how to order in a Cherokee restaurant or tell a Cherokee taxi driver how to take
me to Fifty-Seventh Street and Sutton. The Memrise
course I chose did not include anything as advanced
or helpful as vocabulary or phrases, focusing instead
on the syllabary, a sort of alphabet in which each of
the eighty-five characters represents a syllable instead
of a phoneme.

The Cherokee syllabary was invented in the early
nineteenth century by a Cherokee silversmith variously
named Sequoyah, George Gist, and George Guess,
who had been intrigued by the "talking leaves"—pieces
of paper with peculiar marks—that enabled the white
people to communicate with one another. Sequoyah's
syllabary is the only known instance of a writing system
devised by someone who previously could not read or
write. Some of his symbols resemble letters you know
well, but that coincidence will only trip you up, like

trusting an old friend who is not acting himself. *M*, for instance, sounds like "lu" (think of a **lu**ge going down the mountains of the *M*), and *B* is pronounced "yv" (some users on the site have advised, though not I, that the more vulgar and suggestive you can make your visual or phonetic mnemonic, the easier it is to remember). Other symbols in the syllabary look like an outsider artist's squiggly attempts to evoke an alphabet, for instance ♂, which is a stand-in for the syllable "ma," *Ꭿ*, which is "hi," and Ꮳ, which stands in for "hv."

After presenting his creation to the Cherokee National Council, Sequoyah was accused of witchcraft. According to one report, Sequoyah's first wife had burned a rough draft of his work, but *que sera, sera* (was that French or Italian?). Ultimately the Cherokee Nation adopted the syllabary and gave Sequoyah an award. In 1980 the United States government issued a stamp with his face on it. These nuggets will probably not make you smarter, but maybe this test will.

Here is the entire syllabary. Next to each Cherokee symbol is its English pronunciation. (Note that there is no symbol for "ch," but not to worry, the Cherokee refer to themselves as Tsalagi, spelled Ꮳ Ꮃ Ᏸ, and Chanukah can be spelled Hanukkah, i.e., ᏇnᎱᏫh.) Study the chart for three minutes.

D a	R e	T i	Ꮼ o	O u	i v
S ge	Ꮥ ka	P ge	Y gi	A go	J gu	E gv
Ψ ha	P he	A hi	F ho	Γ hu	Ꮼ hv
W la	δ le	P li	G lo	M lu	ꭹ lv
ơ ma	a me	H mi	ꮟ mo	y mu
Θ na	G hna	Λ ne	h ni	Z no	ꭼ nu	O nv
I qua	ω que	P qui	V quo	ω quu	E quv
U sa	ꭴ s	4 se	b si	Ŧ so	ꭶ su	R sv
L da	W ta	S de	T te	Λ di	J ti	V do	S du	ꮧ dv
δ dla	L tla	L tla	C tli	ꮣ tlo	ꮧ tlu	P tlv
G tsa	V tse	h tsi	K tso	J tsu	ꮯ tsv
G wa	ꮺ we	Θ wi	ꮼ wo	ꮻ wu	6 wv
ꮻ ya	β ye	ꮵ yi	ꭾ yo	G yu	B yv

Got it? Below is a grid of symbols. Circle the items that are authentic Cherokee. Extra credit if you remember the English pronunciations of any of the symbols.

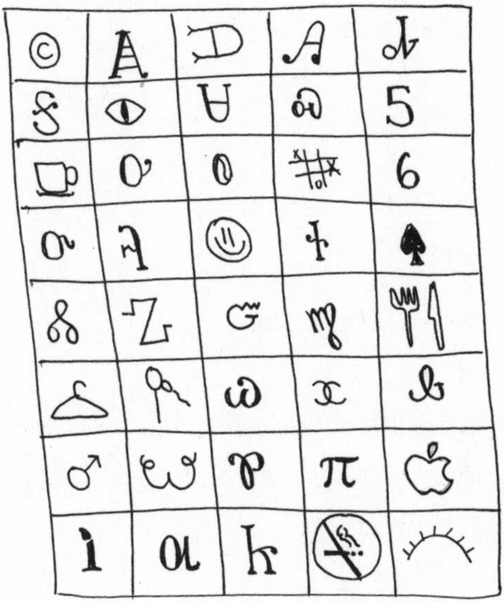

ANSWERS (top to bottom and left to right):

𝐴 = hi

𝟇 = ha

𝔉 = ga

Ա = sa

ꙍ = s

𝒪 = u

𝟇 = wi

𝟔 = wv

𝒪 = nv

ꭹ = lv

Ꮏ = so

Ꮷ = dla

Ꮐ = yu

Ꮖ = que

Ꮕ = hv

Ꮗ = qui

ᎥᎥ = v, but really u, as in *but*, but nasalized

Ꮣ = me

Ꮵ = tsi

SCORING:

Award yourself 1 point for each correct symbol you circled. Deduct 1 point for each incorrect symbol you circled. Ten points for each correct English pronunciation.

   0–4: You call that a hippocampus? More like an amoebacampus.

   5–10: Your hippocampus is now the size of a nectarine.

   10+: Your hippocampus grew so much it can no longer be housed inside your skull and needs to live alone in an apartment.

＊　　　＊　　　＊

Don't say sayonara to the Cherokee just yet. There is one more language quiz. Yes, this is the only book with *two* syllabary-related amusements. I didn't say it was a good thing.

DIRECTIONS:

Convert the following sentences into Cherokee script. You do not have to translate the English words into Cherokee; simply transliterate the Latin characters into Tsalagi phonemes. If there is no corresponding Cherokee character, use English. Spelling counts—a lot. Here's an example:

Gregory Peck is cute = grRAry pRck T𝕺cOᵇᵀ

Does my big toe look infected? = _____?

Where can I buy ointment? = _____?

It needs to be amputated = _____?

Ouch = _____?

Left-footedness runs in my family = _____?

Would you like a mint? = _____?

ANSWERS:

Does my big toe look infected? =
ᏙᎡᏬmy bᎢg tᏬᎡ ᏀᏬk TnfᎡcᏇd?

Where can I buy ointment? =
wᏢrᎡ cᎠn Ꭲ bᏫy ᏬTntᏌnt?

It needs to be amputated =
Ꭲt ᏞᎡdᏬ tᏬ bᎡ DmpᏫᏔᏇd

Ouch = ᏬᏫch

Left-footedness runs in my family =
Ꮥft-fᏬᏬᏇdᏞᏬᏬ rᏫnᏬ Ꭲn my fᎠᎻly

Would you like a mint? =
ᏋᏫld ᏂᏫ ᏢkᎡ Ꭰ Ꮋnt?

Chapter Ten

Shock It to Me, Baby

OUTSIDE PATTY'S BRAIN
During Cranial Electro-Stimulation

Two thousand years ago the Roman emperor Claudius, on the recommendation of his doctor, pressed electric eels against his forehead to ease his headache. For at least twenty minutes a day every day for the past four months, I have fastened a small apparatus to my head, treating my brain to pulses of electricity in hopes that the stimulation will make me more stimulating. Judging from the quality of this paragraph and the length of time it took me to write it, I'm doubtful that the electrons and protons are doing their trick.

The device I've been using—the Fisher Wallace Stimulator—looks like a garage door opener with a tail of two wires. At the end of each wire is an electrode embedded in a sponge the size of an Oreo. These sponges are placed—wet—against your temples and held in position by a navy headband. Touch one of the sponges while the machine is on and you will feel an unpleasant jolt. The electric current comes via two AA batteries and is about 1/1000 the strength used in electroconvulsive therapy, so no need to worry you will turn into a piece of charcoal. Evidently the device has enough oomph, though, to coax the limbic system (boss of your emotions) into stepping up its production of feel-good neurochemicals like serotonin, melatonin, and dopamine while suppressing the release of the feel-bad hormone cortisol.

The stimulator was approved by the FDA for the relief of depression, anxiety, insomnia, and chronic pain. There are lots of clinical studies and meta-analyses backing up these claims, and of course there are doubters, too. Chip Fisher, president of Fisher Wallace Laboratories, LLC, the company that manufactures and distributes the device, told me that it has also been shown to improve eyesight and help with auto-immune diseases, Parkinson's, and ADHD—and he believes it could also make you sharper. Horses who've tried it have fewer episodes of cribbing, headshaking, and anxiety. (Hot tip: Electro-Fury at Saratoga in the fifth race to win.)

I should tell you here and now that I know and like Chip Fisher, so anything negative I may have to say about the Fisher Wallace product, let's blame on Wallace, whom I have never met.

Citing the reverse women-and-children-first principle, I persuaded my boyfriend to try it before I did. Within minutes of turning on the controls, he had a slight headache. Isn't it reassuring when therapy has an effect, even one that is painful or potentially harmful? At least you know the thing is working. When I tried the machine, I saw a faint flickering of light due to the electricity passing through the optical nerve. If there'd been a bulb inside my head, it would have needed changing. Neither of us had any aftereffects (strange dreams are a commonly reported occurrence), but I am still hoping that if I keep the therapy up I will be able to open a garage door telepathically.

Experiment

~~Put your hand in a light socket~~ Never mind.

Chapter Eleven

Name That Tune;
or, This Shouldn't Even Count
as a Chapter if You Ask Me

If you desire to have your offspring grow up to be musical illiterates, then say to them, as my father said to me when, at age eight or so, I protested the injustice of my early-onset piano lessons, "Someday you will thank me." "Oh, no, I won't," I vowed, calculating that even if my father turned out to be right about music's being enriching, the profits could never trump my current agony. Sure enough, today I regret that even "The Itsy Bitsy Spider" is beyond my plinking capacity. I took flute lessons, too, but was allowed to quit when I demonstrated that after three weeks of trying, I couldn't produce a sound. There were also guitar lessons—years' worth that resulted in my knowing seven calypso strums and one song ("Jamaica Farewell"). If I'd had a more successful musical upbringing, would I be smarter now or just more useful at a jam session?

The thesis that music can make you more intelligent was introduced in the 1991 French book *Pourquoi Mozart?: Essay*, and took hold in America two years later when an article in *Nature* magazine stated that listening to one of Wolfie's sonatas augmented spatial reasoning skills for ten to fifteen minutes afterward. The alchemy of the press and public opinion turned this modest claim into: Mozart makes you a Mozart or at least a genius. It wasn't long before hopeful parents were subjecting their newborns to Symphony No. 41 in C Major—and on a farm in Italy, buffalo were exposed to recordings of Mozart three times a day so their milk would make better mozzarella. (Is there such a thing as clever cheese? Is that what "head cheese" is?) The original study was eventually debunked. Subsequent randomized controlled trials found scant evidence that learning to play an instrument has much immediate cognitive benefit. No matter. Eighty percent of Americans persist in their belief that music makes you smarter.

Hold on. They could be right. Evidently the gray matter of those who've studied music is different from that of troglodytes like me. For example, the regions in their cortices that relate to hearing, language production, self-awareness, and executive functioning are larger. What's more, they score higher on their SATs, are more likely to have graduate degrees, and, at least in the case of high school band and orchestra members in Texas in 1998, have lower rates of lifetime alcohol, drug, and tobacco abuse. To what extent can these achievements be explained by a song in the heart? Or could it be that someone who listens to her father is bound for success regardless?

Just in case, as part of my get-smart program, I spent several weeks practicing piano scales, an exercise that must have brought no amount of gladness to my neighbors in 8H. Imagine that I am banging out the following melodies. How many can you identify?

1.

   Dada de-dah!
   Dada de-DAH!...

2.

   Dum dum da dumm.
   Dum dum da-dumm.

Dumm dumm da-dum dum,
Da dumm dumm da dumm…

3.

La-le lad le le-le lah
Le-la lah
Le-la lah
La-le lad le le-le lah
Leh le le lah de lah…

4.

Ahh ah-ah ahhhhh Ahh ah-ah ahhhhhhhhh
Eh eh eh. Eh eh ahh…

5.

Nynah nnah ne nyah nah ne nah na-ah nah

6.

Whine whine, whine whine-o-whine
Whine a whinewhine a whine a whiner…

7.

You-yee you-you yu YOU
You-yee you-you yu YOU…

8.

Haaaah ha ha-ah. Haah ha ha-ha. Hee-hee
hee-hee; hee-hee hee-hee.
Ha he-ha heeee-hah…

9.

Hoo hoo hoo!

10.

To toot-toot-toot toot-toot-toot too too toot,
To toot de to-te TOOT tee...

11.

Bah be bah bah bahh. BAHHH!...

12.

Fting! Ftinng! Ftiiiiinnnng!...

ANSWERS:

1. Beethoven's Fifth Symphony

2. "The Bridal Chorus," aka "Here Comes the Bride"

3. "Mary Had a Little Lamb"

4. "Silent Night"

5. "Blowin' in the Wind" (or any other song as sung by Bob Dylan)

6. "Hey Jude"

7. "Happy Birthday to You"

8. Oscar Mayer commercial for sliced turkey ("Hallelujah Chorus" also accepted)

9. AOL's "You've got mail"

10. The Mister Softee jingle

11. *Hockey Night in Canada* theme song

12. Rosie Wadia, age four, playing Beethoven's Fifth at her first recital on the triangle

SCORING:

1–2: You have no rhythm. Before trying to clap your hands in the audience, hire a tutor.

3–6: Better than André Previn

7–11: If we were playing for real, you would have won a dining room set and an all-expenses-paid trip to Atlantic City.

Perfect score: Quit your job and join a band.

Name That Sound

1. *WhhhssHHHHHwhhhhssHHHHHhhhh HHHH...*

2. *Hrnnnhahnnnh. Hrnnhahnnnh. Snnnghh.*

3. *Pffft, pfft.*

4. *Mwah, mwah. Mwoi, mwoi.*

5. *[Silence]*

ANSWERS:

1. Vacuum cleaner

2. Blowing nose followed by a little sniffling

3. Postprandial eruption of wind

4. Two people social-kissing

5. Sound of one hand clapping

So what if you can't recognize *pfft*s and whooshes? That is what closed captions are for.

Another reason not to despair: A professor of molecular and cellular biology at Harvard, Takao Hensch, is developing a drug, similar to one used to treat epilepsy, that he hopes will make it possible for adults to learn absolute (aka perfect) pitch. This ability to identify and produce a note without any auditory clues is found in only one in ten thousand people, a club that doesn't even include Haydn or Schumann. If you were not born with this prowess, you have a shot at developing it during early childhood when your neural roadways are still extremely malleable. After that, join the rest of us who couldn't say whether the car alarm is blaring in F-sharp minor or B-flat major.

Hensch aims to return our cognitive equipment to its nimble pre-seven-year-old state, where we might not only master perfect pitch, but painlessly and readily pick up new languages and learn how to operate the remote.

Chapter Twelve

Faster, Bigger, More Smarter? The Reckoning

That's not all I did to see if I could get sharper.

I listened to Bach regularly for weeks—and once, in an elevator, Chopin was playing. Or maybe it was "The Girl from Ipanema."

I watched a thirty-six-episode graduate-level series about cosmology—mainly so I could brag about my accomplishment even though the only thing I learned was that everything is either very, very, very, very small or very, very, very, very, very big.

I bought a smartphone.

I ate blueberries because studies show they can protect neurons from fashionably nasty free radicals and excito-toxicity (not as thrilling as its name), and also because blue-berries are featured on just about every list of elixirs to eat.

I ate dark chocolate because one clinical trial found that its compounds help improve your arithmetic abilities, but I probably didn't eat enough because I decided that long division wasn't worth being fat for.

On the ardent recommendation of an acquaintance, I downed Mental Clarity pills. If everyone who's reviewed this product online had truly become as cognitively enhanced as claimed, then cancer would have been cured and someone would have invented earphones that never tangle. The little green pellets, available at health food stores, contain eleven ingredients, if you count nutmeg. The most prevalent, brahmi, is used to treat Alzheimer's disease, ADHD, allergies, irritable bowel syndrome, stress, backache, epilepsy, joint pain, hoarseness, and sexual performance problems in both men and women; indeed, its sundry uses make it the *shalom* of dietary supplements.

I tried to obtain one of the so-called study drugs such as Ritalin, Adderall, and Provigil that temporarily help a user concentrate and improve mental function, and are more popular on college campuses than beer, but I couldn't find anyone who'd part with a tablet. (Tip from a friend who learned the hard way: "If you ever do get your hands on an attention-enhancing drug, make sure you have an attention-deserving project in front of you on your computer screen, for if you are in the middle of shopping for an antique porcelain platter, you are liable to spend the day as the most dedicated and zealous eBay shopper who ever patronized that site.")

I also took fish oil pills because why not.

Overall, I spent so much time trying to improve my brain that I had no time left to use it. Was it worth it?

Nearly four months after my brain was scanned the first time, I returned to the Neuropsychology and Cognitive Neuroscience Lab at Stanford.

A few weeks later, Dr. K (give yourself ten points if you remember that she is the director of the lab at Stanford) e-mailed with renderings of my brain and analyses. The MRI, she reported, indicated that certain regions had increased in volume between 10 and 33 percent. "To be honest," she said over the phone, "the results are very surprising to me. I didn't expect to see this much improvement." Hmm. Could that be a comment on my starting point?

"Thirty-three percent bigger? That's ridiculous," said my boyfriend (to me, not to her). "Your soft tissue would be popping out of your skull." "But what if the areas of expansion were relatively small?" I said. "They're hardly minuscule," he said, looking at the images. He trained as a neuroscientist. He would want you to know that his name is Paul Roossin and that he does not believe size matters. Brain, that is.

I asked Dr. K for clarification. "If parts of my cortex

got bigger," I said, "did other parts get smaller?" "Probably not," she said. "The regions aren't huge percentages. You might have less cerebrospinal fluid or possibly more complex foldings—called gyrification—in the gray matter." No, no, no! By the time you're born—in fact, by the time the fetus is forty weeks old—your brain has all the wrinkles it's ever going to get. As for the cerebrospinal fluid, it courses through ventricles, which are cavities in the brain bringing nutrients and removing wastes from the neural tissue. If my ventricles shrank by 33 percent, this book would likely be posthumous.

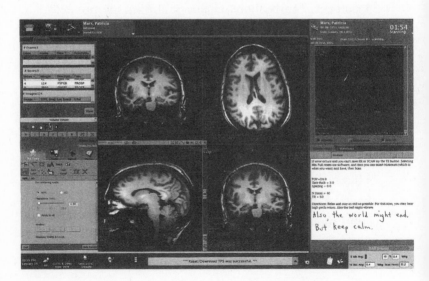

I was also informed that my fMRI revealed a ~~more beautiful, richer, taller, thinner~~ brighter me compared to the dull me of four months earlier. An fMRI, as you will remember if you've become as brilliant as I have, measures brain activity by recording accompanying changes in blood flow while the subject performs a task—in my case the spatial n-back game in which I was asked to recall the positions of dots on grids. Less blood movement means less neural activity means less exertion means either you are executing the task more efficiently or you have had a stroke. How'd I do? Wrote Dr. K, "Your n-back test showed statistically significant change ($p < 0.0001$) in functional brain activation with a 47 percent difference from time 1 to time 2. The attached figure illustrates in cool colors where your brain showed decreased activation and in warm colors where your brain increased activation."

With my swelled head, I e-mailed Paul the good news. He sent me an article entitled "Spiraling Difficulty of Reliably Interpreting Scans of People's Brains."

He has a point.

Now, about my IQ: I probably shouldn't admit this so late in the book, but I don't like information about myself. I don't weigh myself, I wince every tax season when the accountant tells me what I've earned that year, and, don't yell at me, but there are certain

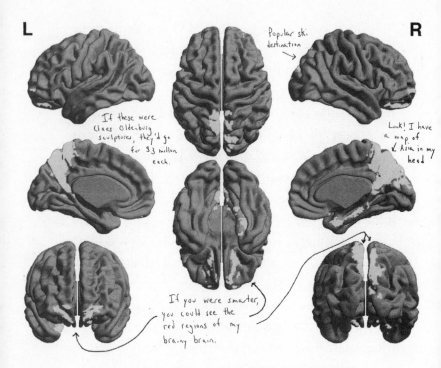

de rigueur medical tests I've never had. Finding out my IQ is something I just can't bear, but knowing whether it went up or down is something I'll have to live with.

The psychologist who had divined my IQ score met me one night at a Japanese restaurant. Before she revealed the verdict, I pretended over the edamame appetizer to be interested in other things besides myself. It was a good sign that she'd ordered edamame,

I deduced—with my fabulous new reasoning powers. Or do I mean induced? Whatever duce it was, edamame is green and that is a nice positive color, as opposed to bad depressing red, which says "Stop, stop, stop, you dumbbell."

The waitress asked whether we'd like some sake. "Yes," said the psychologist. Another encouraging omen. If you were going to deliver unfavorable news, you'd want to be sober, right? Okay, forget the sake argument. "I'm thinking of getting the salmon," the psychologist said.

"The California rolls are supposed to be good here," I said with insistence. Salmon is red, I thought. California is green.

"I'm going to go with the salmon," she said.

Come to think of it, I thought, salmon is orange. Come to think of it, maybe my thinking skills are subpar.

"So?" I said, eyeing the psychologist's folder of papers.

"You have nothing to worry about," she said.

OH NO, OH NO, OH NO, OH NO, OH NO, OH NO, OH NO, OH NO, OH NO, OH NO, OH NO, OH NO!

"Of all the people I've tested," she said, "you are one of the healthiest and cognitively resilient." Who wants to be healthy or resilient? I want to be a genius or at least as smart as Dwight D. Eisenhower. "Your anxiety does not seem to interfere with your cognition," she added, but I was so anxious by now I could barely understand a word she said.

A few of her words did penetrate my mental miasma. Here are some things I remember hearing:

- My best scores were achieved on the verbal parts of the test, which included questions that gauge vocabulary, breadth of general information, comprehension, and ability to glean similarities between two items. The verbal component is the one most contingent on education, which means it cost my parents many thousands of dollars for me to be able to determine out how car is like airplane.
- I am better at naming fruits and vegetables than animals.
- My worst scores were in the area called process-ing speed, which has to do with how quickly you can carry out certain cognitive tasks under pressure. Since I'd been relatively slow the first time I took the test, it was also the index on which I exhibited the most improvement. I will never get a job as a Waring blender.
- May I brag that I scored "very superior" on the Tower of Hanoi test, which is a mathematical

puzzle consisting of disks of different sizes arranged on three rods? The objective is to arrange the disks in size order, largest to smallest, following a specific set of rules. On the other hand, I am weak in block design (which brought down my perceptual reasoning score).

• Even though I consider myself uncommonly adroit when it comes to remembering past and present phone numbers (a useless skill), my working memory is probably not as excellent as Dwight D. Eisenhower's. Ditto my attention faculties.

• Though I am left-handed, my right hand is more coordinated.

• The scores on my sub-tests showed an unusual amount of variability. Most people perform more consistently across the board. For this reason, one general number, I was told, does not capture my overall intelligence.

Enough detail. Did my IQ go up or down or stay the same?

Can you guess whether I've become more or less stupider or have stayed just as stupid as I started? You've known me long enough to venture an answer. While you think about my mental capacity, I'll be drying my hair in the next room if you need me. Turn the page for the results.

ANSWER:

It headed south!

The drop was insignificant, akin to the water weight a dieter loses in the first few days of eating no carbs. Still, that's not what you want to hear after you've spent days and days trying to tune up your thinking machine. Or perhaps it is. If my IQ had gone up a few points, which would have had marginal to no effect on my mental capacities, would I have felt compelled to devote my life to green tea, jumping jacks, Sanskrit, and ukulele lessons? Yes. It's kind of a relief to be free of that. That might be the smartest thought I ever had.

On my way home from dinner that night, I thought about how, in the old days, kings and emperors would send people on missions to find the fountain of youth, the elixir of life. These attendants would travel thousands of miles and come back empty-handed. I accomplished the same in four months without picking up a tropical disease.

Then I realized I lost my hat. It was the second hat

I'd lost that day. Two hats! It could have been worse. At least I still had my head.

Second Opinions from My Friends:

"The delta in your cognitive abilities cannot be properly assessed because there are too many independent variables that are not controlled in this experiment. For example if I were to say you seem smarter to me it could just be that in the past year I have gotten stupider. Proper protocols for this project would have required cryogenically storing all your friends for the year while you did your mishuganah cognitive enhancers. Then defrost us and ask us our views."   *George Hornig*

"As your agent, I can't comment—what if I was funnier?"   *Esther Newberg*

"I would say that you probably can't divide up a check any faster than you ever could."
                    Sybil Sage

"You smarter? That's hilarious. Seriously, that better be hilarious."   *Mark Moffett*

"The challenge of assessing the differential in
your cognitive abilities 10 years ago vs. today
is too daunting to me. Can you still conjugate
the verb *amo*? If so, I can detect no decline.
Likewise, if you are still able to differentiate
'dumb stuff' from 'smart stuff' (something I
could never do), then your cognitive track is a
flat horizontal line."   *Bob Kerrey*

"Changes in your cognitive abilities?
Mmmm...no. But then I didn't know the
colors of my wife's and children's eyes when
they asked me ten years ago. From now on I'll
pay attention."   *Kurt Andersen*

"Have I noticed any particular uptick in
your intelligence from all of your meditation,
Lumosity, etc.? The answer is 'no.' Moreover,
I did notice when we were having lunch
in New York that you were not capable of
explaining Lumosity to me in a way that
made me understand what Lumosity is, but
that may reflect more on me than you. I am
clearly less luminous than you."

                                  Victoria Rostow

"I have definitely detected, since you've started
the brain training, that you send many more
mass emails."   *Lynn Grossman*

"You're exactly the same as you were a year
ago, although you seem to be more concerned
about what I think of your brain than you used
to be."   *Steve Radlauer*

"A mutual friend tells me you have been
making a lot of baskets lately, and braiding
leather. What's with that?"   *Melinda Davis*

"I think that you have become funnier. Not
sure about the other stuff."   *Julie Saul*

"Your brain seems the same in truth."
                                                 Kent Sepkowitz

"There are sparks coming from the top of
your head. It's all right with me if it's all right
with you."   *Melinda Wingate*

"Please send the Cherokee for 'Wish you were
here' (an expression the Cherokees probably
never used)."   *Lorrie Moore*

"This is just an impression, and please ignore
if there's better data—but I feel that since you
started this your breasts have gotten really
perky."   *Philip Weiss*

"Hey, how tall are you anyway? I mean, really?"
                                    Gordon Lish

"Forget memory—you get to my age it's all
about teeth or feet."   *Jennifer Rogers*

Acknowledgments

I feel no end of gratitude to Amanda Brainerd, Melissa Bank, Joan Hornig, George Hornig, Zachariah Hughes, Julie Klam, Cynthia Kling, Susan Lehman, Gerry Ohrstrom, Alexandra Penney, Sarah Stuart, Lucy Teitler, Philip Weiss, and Meg Wolitzer, who contributed ideas and insights. Their brilliances are so formidable I must wear SPF 50 just to talk to any of them on the phone.

Thank you, too, to the brains who study brains: Sherrie All, Shelli Kesler, Faraz Farzin, Alvaro Fernandez, Adam Gazzaley, Kenneth Kosik, Jennifer Medina, Michael Merzenich, Louisa Parks, and Mika Pritchard-Berman. I appreciate the generous time they provided, measuring and explaining.

Six people at Twelve were particularly smart and supportive: S. B. Kleinman, Libby Burton, Elizabeth Kulhanek, Brian McLendon, Mari C. Okuda, and

Paul Samuelson. Many thanks also to the grand and central Jamie Raab at Grand Central.

Of course, my friend and agent, the sage Esther Newberg, gets her own paragraph (and deserves several volumes).

Then there are Janice Marx, Richard Marx, and Sarah Marx, my mother, brother, and sister, respectively, who graciously put up with months and months of telephone calls that went like this: Me—"I can't talk now, I'm working on my book. Bye."

To Paul Roossin, whose neural pathways are too numerous to fathom and whose kindness quarks are even more invaluable, I award a Nobel Prize in Everythingology.

About the Author

After writing this book, Patty Marx got so smart that she changed her name to Patricia Marx.

ABOUT TWELVE

TWELVE

TWELVE was established in August 2005 with the objective of publishing no more than twelve books each year. We strive to publish the singular book, by authors who have a unique perspective and compelling authority. Works that explain our culture; that illuminate, inspire, provoke, and entertain. We seek to establish communities of conversation surrounding our books. Talented authors deserve attention not only from publishers, but from readers as well. To sell the book is only the beginning of our mission. To build avid audiences of readers who are enriched by these works—that is our ultimate purpose.

For more information about forthcoming TWELVE books, please go to www.twelvebooks.com.